SONGS OF THE SOUL

A journey through the Psalms

ROBERT GRIFFITH

GRACE AND TRUTH PUBLISHING
PO Box 338, Gunnedah NSW 2380 Australia
www.graceandtruthpublishing.com.au

All Bible quotes are from the New International Version (NIV) expect where
otherwise stated.

NEW INTERNATIONAL VERSION (NIV), Copyright 1973, 1978 and 1984 by
international Bible Society. Used by permission of Zondervan Publishing House.
All rights reserved.

Other version quotes are from:

AMPLIFIED BIBLE (AMP), Copyright © 1954, 1958, 1962, 1964, 1965, 1987 by
The Lockman Foundation. Used by permission.

ENGLISH STANDARD VERSION (ESV), Copyright © 2001 by Crossway Bibles,
a division of Good News Publishers. Used by permission. All rights reserved.

NEW AMERICAN STANDARD BIBLE (NASB), Copyright © 1960, 1962, 1963, 1968,
1971, 1972, 1973, 1975, 1977, by The Lockman Foundation. Used by permission.

NEW KING JAMES VERSION (NKJV), Copyright © 1979, 1980, 1982, by Thomas
Nelson Inc. Used by permission. All rights reserved.

THE MESSAGE (MSG), by Eugene Peterson, Copyright © 1993, 1994, 1995, 1996,
and 2000. Used by permission of NavPress Publishing Group. All rights reserved.

REVISED STANDARD VERSION (RSV), Copyright © 1973, by Thomas Nelson Inc.
Used by permission. All rights reserved.

ISBN 978-1-7635504-6-9

INTRODUCTION

The Book of Psalms has been described as the heart of the Bible, and for very good reason. Here we find the full range of human experience poured out before a holy, merciful, and faithful God. From the soaring heights of praise to the depths of despair, from raw cries for justice to serene meditations on God's character, the Psalms offer us words when our own may fail.

Songs of the Soul was born out of a deep desire to walk slowly and reverently through this sacred collection - one Psalm at a time. It is important that you read each Psalm first before exploring its accompanying reflection here. This is not a commentary, but a focused meditation. So, the goal here is not so much to analyse the Psalms academically, but to encounter them devotionally.

Every page has been prayerfully crafted to draw attention to the central truth of each Psalm, to highlight its relevance for our lives today, and to encourage personal worship and spiritual growth.

The language used is intentionally clear and accessible, making this book suitable for daily devotions, Bible study groups, or for anyone seeking to deepen their appreciation of God's Word.

Each Psalm stands alone, yet all are part of a larger symphony. As you turn these pages, you will move from laments to hymns, from royal declarations to wisdom sayings. You'll hear David's personal prayers, the nation's communal songs, and anonymous voices crying out in faith.

Through it all, one truth resounds: God is worthy of our praise - always, everywhere, and in every circumstance. As you explore the Psalms, may you find comfort in your pain, direction in your confusion, and renewed joy in your worship.

Take your time. Linger with each 'song of the soul' and let the ancient words become your own … and may your heart, like the Psalmist's, be stirred to say, *"I will praise the Lord all my life; I will sing praise to my God as long as I live."* (Psalm 146:2)

PSALM 1

Author: Unknown (possibly David)

Theme: Two ways to live - blessedness or ruin.

Summary:

Psalm 1 opens the entire book with a stark contrast between the life of the righteous and the life of the wicked. The righteous person is described as someone who does not walk in step with the wicked, stand in the way of sinners, or sit in the seat of mockers. Instead, this person finds joy in God's law and then meditates on it day and night. This steady, spiritual focus is compared to a tree planted by streams of water - deeply rooted, continually nourished, and always fruitful.

By contrast, the wicked have no such stability. They are like chaff blown away by the wind - useless, weightless, and impermanent. They will not stand in the judgment, nor will they be counted among the righteous.

The Psalm closes with this profound assurance: *"For the Lord watches over the way of the righteous, but the way of the wicked leads to destruction."*

This Psalm is not simply good moral instruction - it is a spiritual compass. It invites us to orient our lives around God's truth, offering us a vision of flourishing that the world cannot imitate. It sets the tone for all the Psalms by reminding us clearly that our response to God's Word shapes every aspect of our life.

Key Verse: (v.2)
"But whose delight is in the law of the Lord, and who meditates on his law, day and night."

Application:

Where we place our trust determines the fruit of our lives. Psalm 1 calls us to delight in God's Word, not as duty but as a source of life. The way of the righteous is not easier, but it is grounded, guided, and ultimately watched over by the Lord Himself.

PSALM 2

Author: David (confirmed in Acts 4:25)

Theme: God's sovereign rule over rebellious nations.

Summary:

Psalm 2 opens with a vivid image of global rebellion. The nations rage, rulers conspire, and kings unite in defiance against the Lord and His Anointed. Their cry - *"Let us break their chains and throw off their shackles"*- expresses humanity's deep resistance to God's authority. But God remains unshaken. He sits in the heavens and laughs, not in a mocking way, but rather in quiet, sovereign confidence.

God then declares: *"You are my Son; today I have become your Father."* These words speak prophetically of Jesus Christ, God's ultimate Anointed One. He will inherit the nations, rule with authority, and bring justice to the earth.

The Psalm concludes with a sober warning and a gracious invitation. Earthly rulers are urged to act wisely - to serve the Lord with fear and to rejoice with trembling. They are told to *"kiss the Son,"* an act of reverence and surrender, lest His wrath break out. Yet, the final line offers great hope: *"Blessed are all who take refuge in him."*

Psalm 2 is a warning and a promise, reminding us that God's purposes cannot be overthrown. Christ reigns, not just in heaven, but ultimately over every nation and heart.

Key Verse: (v.12)

"Blessed are all who take refuge in him."

Application:

In a world that often rejects God's authority, Psalm 2 invites us to a better response - humble submission. True peace comes not through autonomy, but through surrender to Jesus, the eternal King who rules with justice, mercy, and grace.

PSALM 3

Author: David

Theme: Confidence in God during times of personal crisis.

Summary:

David wrote this Psalm while fleeing from his son Absalom. This was one of the darkest and most dangerous moments in David's life. Surrounded by enemies and betrayed by his own child, David cries out to God in distress. *"Lord, how many are my foes!"* he begins, expressing a sense of being overwhelmed - not only by numbers but by the cruel taunt that *"God will not deliver him."*

Yet amid this turmoil, David's tone quickly shifts from fear to faith. He declares, *"But you, Lord, are a shield around me, my glory, the One who lifts my head high."* Even as his world collapses, David affirms that God is his protector and source of honour. He lies down and sleeps, knowing that the Lord sustains him. Sleep becomes a testimony of faith in a God who does not slumber.

David awakens with boldness, declaring he will not fear - even if tens of thousands rise against him. He calls on the Lord to arise and deliver, and he remembers past victories, trusting that God will again defeat his enemies.

Psalm 3 reminds us that faith is not the absence of trouble, but trust in the midst of it. David models how we can respond to crisis not with despair, but with confidence in God's character.

Key Verse (v.3)

"But you, Lord, are a shield around me, my glory, the One who lifts my head high."

Application:

When fear threatens to take over, we can find rest by trusting in God's protection. Like David, we are invited to bring our burdens to the Lord and sleep in peace, knowing He watches over us and delivers us in His time.

PSALM 4

Author: David

Theme: Finding peace by trusting God in troubling times.

Summary:

Psalm 4 is an evening prayer that reveals David's deep trust in God during times of pressure and slander. He begins by calling on the *"God of my righteousness,"* recalling how God has given him relief in past distress and asking for that same mercy now. David is being maligned by his enemies, but he confidently reminds them that *"the Lord has set apart his faithful servant for himself."* He knows that God hears him when he calls.

David offers wise counsel to those who are angry or tempted to sin: *"Tremble and do not sin; when you are on your beds, search your hearts and be silent."* In other words, don't act out of emotion - pause, reflect, and always trust God.

Others cry out for external signs of goodness or success, but David's joy comes from something far deeper: the presence and favour of God. His confidence leads to true peace. He ends with one of the most comforting declarations in Scripture: *"In peace I will lie down and sleep, for you alone, Lord, make me dwell in safety."*

Key Verse: (v.8)

"In peace I will lie down and sleep, for you alone, Lord, make me dwell in safety."

Application:

In a world so filled with anxiety, conflict, and sleepless nights, Psalm 4 invites just us to rest - not because all our problems are solved, but because God is our protector. When slandered or opposed, we are called not to fight back in bitterness, but to trust the God who sets His people apart and answers when we call. Peace comes when we place our security in the Lord, not in circumstances. Like David, we can lie down each night knowing the One who watches over us never sleeps.

PSALM 5

Author: David

Theme: Seeking God's guidance and justice in the morning.

Summary:

Psalm 5 is a morning prayer in which David lifts his voice to God and commits his day to Him. He begins with urgency: *"Listen to my words, Lord, consider my lament."* David is crying out with the raw emotion of someone surrounded by threats. He brings his urgent requests before God and waits expectantly.

David then reflects on God's character. He knows that the Lord is not indifferent to evil. God takes no pleasure in wickedness, arrogance, or deceit, and He will ultimately judge those who persist in rebellion. These are not just observations - they're assurances.

David prays for guidance: *"Lead me, Lord, in your righteousness because of my enemies - make your way straight before me."* He seeks not just protection, but moral direction. David also prays that the lies and rebellion of the wicked would be exposed.

He knows their hearts are filled with destruction, and he asks God to hold them accountable. But he ends with confidence and joy because those who take refuge in the Lord will rejoice. God blesses the righteous and surrounds them with favour as with a shield.

Key Verse: (v.11)

"But let all who take refuge in you be glad; let them ever sing for joy."

Application:

Begin each day by seeking God in prayer. In a world filled with deception and pride, it's essential to realign our hearts with God's truth. Like David, we should bring our concerns and requests before the Lord, trusting in His justice and guidance. Those who take refuge in Him can walk with joy, knowing they are shielded by His favour.

PSALM 6

Author: David

Theme: A cry for mercy in the midst of suffering.

Summary:

Psalm 6 is the first of seven 'penitential Psalms,' where David expresses deep sorrow for sin and overwhelming distress. He begins with a heartfelt plea: *"Lord, do not rebuke me in your anger or discipline me in your wrath."* His language reveals that he feels crushed not just physically, but also spiritually and emotionally. David's bones ache, his soul is in anguish.

This is a moment of vulnerability for David. He pours out his heart in raw honesty, confessing his weakness and pleading for deliverance. *"Turn, Lord, and deliver me; save me because of your unfailing love."* That phrase - *"unfailing love"* - is central. David doesn't appeal to his own righteousness, but to God's character.

In verses 5 to 7, David vividly describes his grief. His nights are filled with weeping. His bed is drenched with tears. His eyes grow weak with sorrow. Then comes a turning point. Suddenly, David's tone shifts. He declares, *"The Lord has heard my cry for mercy; the Lord accepts my prayer."* It's as if in the act of praying, David regains assurance that God is listening. Psalm 6 teaches us that believers can be overwhelmed and faithful at the same time.

Key Verse: (v. 9)

"The Lord has heard my cry for mercy; the Lord accepts my prayer."

Application:

When you feel broken - whether physically, emotionally, or spiritually - do what David did: run to God, not away from Him. Cry out with honesty. God can handle your sorrow, your guilt, and your pain.

Like David, you may not feel immediate relief, but you can be confident that your prayer is heard. In His mercy, God draws near to those who seek Him with a humble heart.

PSALM 7

Author: David

Theme: God is a righteous Judge who vindicates the innocent.

Summary:

Psalm 7 is a passionate prayer for vindication. David is being falsely accused, and rather than retaliate, he brings his case before the highest court - God's own judgment seat. *"Lord my God, I take refuge in you; save and deliver me from all who pursue me,"* he begins. He trusts that God sees all, knows all, and will act in righteousness. He says, in effect, *"If I am guilty, let my enemy overtake me."* That kind of transparency comes only from someone who knows he is innocent and who trusts God completely. David is not asking for special treatment.

He then calls on God to rise against the wickedness around him, to decree judgment. David affirms that God judges the people with equity and examines the minds and hearts of all. God is not passive. He is actively involved in defending the righteous.

David describes God preparing for judgment like a warrior sharpening his sword. Those who do evil dig traps for others but fall into them themselves. This poetic justice, where sin rebounds on the sinner, is a theme often seen in the Psalms.

David finishes by saying, *"I will give thanks to the Lord because of his righteousness; I will sing the praises of the name of the Lord Most High."* He trusts that justice will be done.

Key Verse: (v.10)
"My shield is God Most High, who saves the upright in heart."

Application:

When you're wrongly accused or treated unfairly, resist the urge to seek revenge. Bring your situation to God, your righteous Judge. He sees your heart and defends those who walk in integrity. Trust Him to bring justice in His perfect time.

Psalm 8

Author: David

Theme: God's majestic glory and humanity's honoured place.

Summary:
Psalm 8 is a song of praise that marvels at the greatness of God and the dignity He has bestowed on humanity. It opens and closes with the same exclamation: *"Lord, our Lord, how majestic is your name in all the earth!"* This Psalm reflects on the paradox that the Creator of the universe really cares for insignificant humans.

David looks up at the night sky, the moon and stars, and is filled with awe. Compared to the vastness of the cosmos, humans seem small. *"What is mankind that you are mindful of them, human beings that you care for them?"* he asks. It's a humbling question. Yet the answer reveals a profound truth: God has given humanity a place of honour.

Humans are described as being made *"a little lower than the angels,"* crowned with glory and honour. We are entrusted with dominion over the earth - over all creatures, from domesticated animals to birds and fish.

In Hebrews 2, this Psalm is applied to Jesus, showing that Christ, the true Son of Man, fulfils the destiny originally given to all humanity. He reigns in perfection where we have all failed, restoring our purpose and glory through His redemptive work.

Key Verse: (v.4)
"What is mankind that you are mindful of them, human beings that you care for them?"

Application:
You matter deeply to God. Even though you may at times feel insignificant, He has crowned you with honour and entrusted you with purpose. Praise Him for the majesty of His creation - and the miracle that He has made you a vital part of it.

PSALM 9

Author: David

Theme: Praising God for justice and deliverance.

Summary:

Psalm 9 is a song of thanksgiving in which David praises God for His righteous rule and justice on behalf of the oppressed. It begins with personal gratitude: *"I will give thanks to you, Lord, with all my heart; I will tell of all your wonderful deeds."* David celebrates victories over enemies, declaring that it is God who upholds his cause and judges righteously.

David encourages those who know the Lord to trust Him and seek Him in prayer. He says, *"Those who know your name trust in you, for you, Lord, have never forsaken those who seek you."* The Psalmist calls the people to praise God and proclaim His deeds, especially His defence of the afflicted.

The second half of the Psalm shifts to petition. David asks the Lord to act again on behalf of the afflicted. He says, *"Arise, Lord, do not let mortals triumph."* He appeals to God's justice to bring down the wicked and remind humanity of their frailty.

David closes with a plea for accountability: *"Strike them with terror, Lord; let the nations know they are only mortal."* This is not a cry for vengeance but for justice - to put evil in its place.

Key Verse: (v.9)

"The Lord is a refuge for the oppressed, a stronghold in times of trouble."

Application:

Psalm 9 reminds us that God sees and responds to injustice. He is not passive in the face of evil. When you feel overwhelmed or wronged, turn to Him. Praise Him for what He has done and trust Him for what He will do. Let your heart be anchored in His righteousness and your voice be part of the testimony of His faithfulness.

PSALM 10

Author: Not specified

Theme: God sees injustice and will defend the oppressed.

Summary:

Psalm 10 opens with a heartfelt question many have asked in times of distress: *"Why, Lord, do you stand far off? Why do you hide yourself in times of trouble?"* The Psalmist expresses a deep frustration at the apparent success of wicked people. They are arrogant, deceitful, greedy, and hostile to God. *"In his pride the wicked man does not seek him; in all his thoughts there is no room for God."* They boast, curse, and ambush the innocent.

These powerful words reflect a world where justice feels delayed and the vulnerable suffer without recourse. The wicked prey on the weak, thinking themselves above accountability. But the tone of the Psalm begins to shift.

The writer calls out to God: *"Arise, Lord! Lift up your hand, O God. Do not forget the helpless."* He appeals to God's character - His justice, His care for the afflicted, His power to defend. The Psalmist knows that despite appearances, the Lord always sees everything: *"But you, God, see the trouble of the afflicted; you consider their grief and take it in hand."* The Psalm ends with renewed confidence. God is King forever. Though evil seems strong, it will not last.

Key Verse: (v.14)

"But you, God, see the trouble of the afflicted; you consider their grief and take it in hand."

Application:

Psalm 10 reminds us that while injustice may seem to go unchecked, God is never indifferent. He sees. He knows. And in His time, He will act. When evil seems to triumph, we are invited not to despair, but to pray boldly and trust deeply in the God who defends the helpless and brings down the arrogant.

PSALM 11

Author: David

Theme: Trusting God's justice when foundations are shaken.

Summary:

Psalm 11 opens with a bold declaration of trust: *"In the Lord I take refuge."* David is being urged to flee - perhaps by fearful advisors - who warn him that the wicked are preparing to shoot from the shadows. *"When the foundations are being destroyed,"* they ask, *"what can the righteous do?"* It's a deeply relevant question. When moral and social structures collapse, when justice seems absent, when chaos reigns - what can those who honour God do? David's answer is clear: look up. *"The Lord is in his holy temple; the Lord is on his heavenly throne."* God is not shaken. He still rules.

David affirms that God observes everyone closely. *"His eyes examine them."* He tests the righteous, and He hates with passion the deeds of the wicked - those who love violence will face His judgment. The image is intense: fiery coals, burning sulphur, a scorching wind. God's justice is not abstract - it is active, deliberate, and final.

The Psalm closes with hope: *"For the Lord is righteous, he loves justice; the upright will see his face."* In the end, those who trust God will not be forgotten or overlooked. They will experience His presence and favour.

Key Verse: (v.3)
"When the foundations are being destroyed, what can the righteous do?"

Application:

In times of cultural confusion, political corruption, or personal fear, Psalm 11 calls us to stand firm in God's character. We may feel tempted to flee or despair, but our confidence is not in the stability of earthly systems - it is in the unchanging justice of God, who sees all and will not forsake the upright.

PSALM 12

Author: David

Theme: God's pure words in a corrupt and deceptive world.

Summary:
Psalm 12 is a cry for help in a society overrun with lies and flattery. David laments that the faithful have vanished and that everyone lies to their neighbour. *"They flatter with their lips but harbour deception in their hearts."* Truth has become rare, and arrogance abounds.

David doesn't just complain - he prays. He asks the Lord to silence proud lips and to defend the oppressed. The wicked boast, *"We own our lips - who is our master?"* They see no higher authority, no accountability. But David knows that God hears. *"Because the poor are plundered and the needy groan, I will now arise,"* declares the Lord.

In contrast to human speech, which is manipulative and false, God's words are pure: *"like silver refined in a crucible, like gold refined seven times."* His promises are trustworthy and true. While wickedness may seem pervasive, God's Word remains a refuge.

David ends with a realistic observation: *"The wicked freely strut about when what is vile is honoured by the human race."* Yet his trust remains in the God who guards His people.

Key Verse: (v.6)
"And the words of the Lord are flawless, like silver purified in a crucible, like gold refined seven times."

Application:
In a world where deception often feels normal, Psalm 12 reminds us to cling to the truth of God's Word. His promises are pure, tested, and unchanging. Even when wickedness appears to dominate, we are not without hope - we have a God who hears the groans of the oppressed and speaks words that never fail.

PSALM 13

Author: David

Theme: Wrestling with God's silence and reaffirming trust.

Summary:

Psalm 13 gives voice to a deeply human experience: the silence of God in times of crisis. David opens with a lament that's honest and desperate: *"How long, Lord? Will you forget me forever? How long will you hide your face from me?"* The repetition emphasizes his pain. He feels abandoned, and spiritually exhausted.

David's anguish is not only emotional but also mental. *"How long must I wrestle with my thoughts and day after day have sorrow in my heart?"* This is the inner turmoil of someone who is trying to remain faithful but feels overwhelmed by his circumstances. Yet despite the silence and struggle, David does not stop praying. He pleads with God to answer: *"Look on me and answer, Lord my God. Give light to my eyes, or I will sleep in death."* David doesn't just want relief - he wants restored fellowship.

The turning point comes in verses 5 and 6. Even though his situation hasn't visibly changed, David's posture shifts: *"But I trust in your unfailing love; my heart rejoices in your salvation."* Psalm 13 teaches that faith is not the absence of questions, but the choice to trust even when the answers are not clear.

Key Verse: (v.5)

"But I trust in your unfailing love; my heart rejoices in your salvation."

Application:

When God feels distant and life is dark, keep praying. Bring your doubts and pain to Him honestly. Faith doesn't silence our questions - it lifts them into God's presence. Like David, you can choose to trust God's love and remember His goodness, even before your circumstances change. In the valley of silence, His grace still sustains.

PSALM 14

Author: David

Theme: Human corruption and the hope of God's intervention.

Summary:

Psalm 14 is a sobering assessment of the human condition apart from God. It begins with a blunt statement: *"The fool says in his heart, 'There is no God.'"* This is not just atheism in a modern sense - it's moral defiance. The *"fool"* here is someone who lives as if God does not exist, rejecting His authority and accountability.

David continues by describing the scope of human corruption. *"They are corrupt, their deeds are vile; there is no one who does good."* God looks down from heaven to see if anyone seeks Him, and He finds that all have turned away. This echoes themes later found in Romans 3, where Paul quotes this Psalm.

The wicked don't just ignore God - they actively oppress His people. *"They devour my people as though eating bread,"* David writes, illustrating their cruelty and lack of conscience. Yet he reassures us: *"God is present in the company of the righteous."*

The Psalm ends with a longing and a promise: *"Oh, that salvation for Israel would come out of Zion!"* This prophetic hope points forward to the ultimate deliverance in Jesus Christ, the true Redeemer who brings joy to His people and restores what sin has broken.

Key Verse: (v.5)
"The Lord is present in the company of the righteous."

Application:

Psalm 14 reminds us that human nature left to itself turns from God. But it also affirms that God is not distant - He is with those who seek Him. When the world mocks faith and honours wickedness, take courage: the Lord is your refuge, and salvation is assured in Him.

PSALM 15

Author: David

Theme: The character of one who lives in God's presence.

Summary:

Psalm 15 begins with a profound question: *"Lord, who may dwell in your sacred tent? Who may live on your holy mountain?"* This is not about physical access to a temple - it's more about spiritual communion with God. David is asking: who is truly at home with the Lord? The answer is both practical and deeply ethical. *"The one whose walk is blameless, who does what is righteous, who speaks the truth from their heart."*

The Psalm lists qualities that reflect a life of integrity: honesty, loyalty, humility, and justice. The blameless person does not slander or gossip. They keep their word, even when it's costly. They treat others with fairness and refuse to exploit the innocent. Importantly, the Psalm doesn't suggest perfection. Rather, it reveals the kind of life shaped by God's presence. David includes a note about honour: this person *"honours those who fear the Lord"* and *"despises a vile person."* Psalm 15 challenges us to value character above status.

The final verse has an assurance: *"Whoever does these things will never be shaken."* This doesn't mean life is trouble-free - but that the person who lives with integrity will have a firm foundation.

Key Verse: (v.1)

"Lord, who may dwell in your sacred tent? Who may live on your holy mountain?"

Application:

Psalm 15 challenges us to examine the way we live before God. Are our lives marked by truth, integrity, and compassion? Do we honour God in our speech, relationships, and commitments? Living in God's presence transforms our character - and those who walk uprightly can stand firm even in uncertain times.

PSALM 16

Author: David

Theme: Security, joy, and eternal hope in God's presence.

Summary:

Psalm 16 is a declaration of confidence and contentment in God. David opens with a simple but heartfelt plea: *"Keep me safe, my God, for in you I take refuge."* From that foundation of trust, he expresses his full allegiance: *"Apart from you I have no good thing."* This is not mere religious duty - it's a joyful dependence.

David acknowledges the righteous as his companions and rejects the path of those who pursue other gods. He chooses a different inheritance: *"Lord, you alone are my portion and my cup; you make my lot secure."* This shows a deep satisfaction in God's provision.

One of the most powerful affirmations comes in verse 8: *"I keep my eyes always on the Lord. With him at my right hand, I will not be shaken."* This focus leads to inner peace, joy, and confidence in both life and death.

Psalm 16 culminates in a powerful prophetic promise: *"You will not abandon me to the realm of the dead, nor will you let your faithful one see decay."* Quoted in Acts 2 and Acts 13, this verse points directly to Jesus and His resurrection. In Christ, we too are given hope beyond the grave.

Key Verse: (v.11)

"You make known to me the path of life; you will fill me with joy in your presence, with eternal pleasures at your right hand."

Application:

Psalm 16 calls us to anchor our identity, joy, and security in God alone. Earthly pleasures fade, but life in God's presence brings lasting delight. Whether in life or death, we have nothing to fear when the Lord is our portion and our guide. Fix your eyes on Him - and you will not be shaken.

PSALM 17

Author: David

Theme: A cry for justice and protection from the wicked.

Summary:

In this passionate prayer from David, he seeks vindication and deliverance from enemies who threaten his life. He begins with a plea: *"Hear me, Lord, my plea is just; listen to my cry."* David appeals to God's fairness and omniscience, saying that God has tested his heart and found no deceit. He doesn't claim perfection, but he does claim sincerity.

David is determined to follow the Lord's ways. *"My steps have held to your paths; my feet have not stumbled."* This isn't self-righteousness - it's confidence that he has lived with integrity amid hostile opposition. He calls on God to *"show the wonder of your great love,"* to save by His right hand those who take refuge in Him.

David describes his enemies as arrogant, unfeeling, and deadly. *"They have tracked me down; they now surround me."* He contrasts their earthly focus with his own eternal hope. *"They are satisfied with children and leave their wealth to their little ones,"* he observes. But David's desire goes far beyond temporary success: *"As for me, I will be vindicated and will see your face; when I awake, I will be satisfied with seeing your likeness."*

Key Verse: (v.8)
"Keep me as the apple of your eye; hide me in the shadow of your wings."

Application:

Psalm 17 teaches us to bring our need for justice and protection directly to God. When faced with unfair treatment or looming threats, we can cry out to the One who sees our hearts and defends the righteous. Earthly gains fade, but the joy of seeing God's face lasts forever.

PSALM 18

Author: David

Theme: God's powerful deliverance and faithful love.

Summary:

Psalm 18, one of David's longest Psalms, is a song of victory and thanksgiving after God delivered him from all his enemies, including Saul. He begins with personal devotion: *"I love you, Lord, my strength."* Then he praises God as his rock, fortress, and deliverer - his shield and stronghold.

David describes how, in distress, he cried to God. From His heavenly temple, God heard his voice. What follows is a majestic description of divine intervention. *"He reached down from on high and took hold of me; he drew me out of deep waters."* God rescues David not just from danger but from despair. He brings him into a spacious place because *"he delighted in me."*

He reflects on the importance of righteousness and obedience - not perfection, but a heart aligned with God. *"To the faithful you show yourself faithful,"* he says. David celebrates how God equips him, strengthens him, trains his hands for battle, and gives him victory over his enemies.

The Psalm ends with David proclaiming God's greatness. *"The Lord lives! Praise be to my Rock!"* He acknowledges that every triumph comes from the Lord.

Key Verse: (v.16)
"He reached down from on high and took hold of me; he drew me out of deep waters."

Application:

Psalm 18 reminds us that our God is mighty to save. When we face overwhelming odds or feel surrounded by darkness, we can call on the One who hears from heaven and comes to rescue. His power is unmatched, His love unwavering, and His faithfulness everlasting.

PSALM 19

Author: David

Theme: God reveals Himself through creation and His Word.

Summary:

Psalm 19 is a glorious reflection on how God speaks to humanity - first through the natural world and then through His written Word. *"The heavens declare the glory of God; the skies proclaim the work of his hands."* Day and night, without a single word spoken, the universe testifies to God's greatness. David describes how the sun rises like a bridegroom and runs its course with joy, warming everything under its heat. This imagery reveals the power and reach of God's voice through creation.

Then the Psalm shifts focus to God's law: *"The law of the Lord is perfect, refreshing the soul."* David uses six terms - law, statutes, precepts, commands, fear, and decrees - all describing different aspects of God's Word. It is trustworthy, right, radiant, pure, firm, and righteous. It brings joy, enlightenment, and wisdom.

David treasures God's Word more than gold and finds it sweeter than honey. It warns, it corrects, and it blesses those who follow it. He acknowledges his own hidden faults and asks God for cleansing and protection from sin. The Psalm closes with a prayer that his words and thoughts would be pleasing to God: *"Lord, my Rock and my Redeemer."*

Key Verse: (v.14)

"May these words of my mouth and this meditation of my heart be pleasing in your sight, Lord, my Rock and my Redeemer."

Application:

Psalm 19 invites us to listen - to the voice of creation and the voice of Scripture. God is speaking, both through the world He made and the Word He gave. Let His glory stir your worship, and let His truth shape your life. Seek not just knowledge, but transformation, through His Word.

PSALM 20

Author: David

Theme: A prayer of blessing and victory before battle.

Summary:

Psalm 20 is a royal Psalm - a prayer offered on behalf of the king as he prepares for battle. It begins with blessings: *"May the Lord answer you when you are in distress… May he send you help from the sanctuary and grant you support from Zion."* David prays that God would remember the king's sacrifices and give him the desires of his heart.

This is not a selfish wish list but a longing for God's will and favour in a moment of national vulnerability. The people express collective faith in God's power: *"Now this I know: The Lord gives victory to his anointed."* God will answer from His heavenly sanctuary and bring triumph through His mighty hand.

The most famous verse follows: *"Some trust in chariots and some in horses, but we trust in the name of the Lord our God."* Military strength may impress, but it cannot guarantee success. Victory comes from the Lord alone.

The enemies may collapse and fall, but those who trust in God rise and stand firm. The Psalm ends with a final plea: *"Lord, give victory to the king! Answer us when we call!"*

Key Verse: (v.7)

"Some trust in chariots and some in horses, but we trust in the name of the Lord our God."

Application:

Psalm 20 reminds us that real security will never come from power, planning, or possessions - but from trusting in God.

When facing battles - spiritual or physical - put your hope in the Lord. Lift your voice in prayer and look to Him for victory.

PSALM 21

Author: David

Theme: Gratitude for God's strength, favour, and victory.

Summary:
Psalm 21 is a song of praise celebrating the Lord's faithfulness to the king. It follows naturally from Psalm 20, which was a prayer for victory. Now David rejoices in answered prayer: *"The king rejoices in your strength, Lord. How great is his joy in the victories you give!"* God has granted the king's desires, blessings, and long life.

David makes clear that it is God - not military power or personal skill - who brings victory. *"Through the victories you gave, his glory is great."* The king rejoices not in what he has achieved, but in what the Lord has done.

Central to this Psalm is trust. *"For the king trusts in the Lord; through the unfailing love of the Most High he will not be shaken."* Trust is the anchor of security, and God's love is the source of lasting stability.

But the Psalm also includes a warning to the wicked. Those who oppose God and His anointed will be confronted and consumed. His hand will seize His enemies, and fire will devour them. The Psalm closes with renewed praise: *"Be exalted in your strength, Lord; we will sing and praise your might."* David's heart is full - not with pride, but with worship.

Key Verse: (v.7)
"For the king trusts in the Lord; through the unfailing love of the Most High he will not be shaken."

Application:
When God grants success, we must respond with gratitude, not arrogance. Psalm 21 teaches us to celebrate victories by giving honour to the One who makes them possible. Trust in the Lord brings strength, and His unfailing love secures us far beyond the temporary triumphs of life.

PSALM 22

Author: David

Theme: A cry of suffering that points prophetically to Christ.

Summary:

Psalm 22 begins with a haunting line later spoken by Jesus on the cross: *"My God, my God, why have you forsaken me?"* David expresses deep anguish, feeling abandoned despite his cries for help. He recalls how God rescued his ancestors but now feels personally forsaken: *"I am a worm and not a man, scorned by everyone, despised by the people."*

Mockers ridicule his faith: *"He trusts in the Lord... Let the Lord rescue him."* These words, too, echo at Calvary. David describes intense physical and emotional suffering - his strength is dried up, his bones are out of joint, his heart melts like wax.

The imagery of crucifixion becomes even more vivid: *"They pierce my hands and my feet... They divide my clothes among them and cast lots for my garment."* Though written centuries before Jesus, this Psalm powerfully anticipates His passion.

Yet the Psalm does not end in despair. David pleads for help: *"But you, Lord, do not be far from me* - and then turns to praise. The Psalm ends with a vision of the future: *"They will proclaim his righteousness, declaring to a people yet unborn: He has done it!"* These final words parallel Jesus' cry, *"It is finished."*

Key Verse: (v.31)

"They will proclaim his righteousness, declaring to a people yet unborn: He has done it!"

Application:

Psalm 22 reminds us that God hears even when He seems silent. In our pain, we can cry out honestly like David - and like Jesus. This Psalm anchors our suffering in a larger story: the suffering of Christ that brings redemption. God never wastes pain, and His purposes will prevail.

PSALM 23

Author: David

Theme: God's shepherding care and eternal presence.

Summary:

Psalm 23 is one of the most beloved passages in all Scripture - a declaration of trust in the Lord as Shepherd. *"The Lord is my shepherd, I lack nothing."* David begins with a personal, intimate statement of confidence. God leads, provides, protects, and restores. *"He makes me lie down in green pastures, he leads me beside quiet waters, he refreshes my soul."* The imagery is tender and sustaining. Even in dark valleys - symbolic of danger, fear, and even death - David fears no evil because God is with him. *"Your rod and your staff, they comfort me."*

The tone shifts from pastoral to royal: *"You prepare a table before me in the presence of my enemies."* God doesn't just rescue - He honours. The anointing with oil and the overflowing cup signify blessing, dignity, and joy. David concludes with a powerful promise: *"Surely your goodness and love will follow me all the days of my life, and I will dwell in the house of the Lord forever."* This is not wishful thinking - it's a confident declaration of God's eternal faithfulness.

Psalm 23 reveals a God who walks beside us in green pastures and dark valleys alike. It is a Psalm of assurance, not because life is easy, but because the Shepherd never leaves.

Key Verse: (v.4)

"Even though I walk through the darkest valley, I will fear no evil, for you are with me."

Application:

Let Psalm 23 shape how you see life. You are not alone - God is leading, protecting, and pursuing you with His goodness and love. Whether you're in rest or trial, joy or grief, He is present. Trust your Shepherd - and dwell in His house forever.

PSALM 24

Author: David

Theme: God's sovereign rule.

Summary:

Psalm 24 begins with a grand declaration of divine ownership: *"The earth is the Lord's, and everything in it, the world, and all who live in it."* God is not a regional deity - He is the sovereign Creator of all. He founded the earth and rules over it completely. The Psalm then asks a crucial question: *"Who may ascend the mountain of the Lord? Who may stand in his holy place?"* The answer is moral and spiritual: *"The one who has clean hands and a pure heart, who does not trust in an idol or swear by a false god."* Entering God's presence requires integrity, sincerity, and undivided devotion.

Those who seek God this way receive blessing and vindication. *"Such is the generation of those who seek him, who seek your face, God of Jacob."* This is not about religious performance but genuine pursuit.

The final section is a triumphant call: *"Lift up your heads, you gates... that the King of glory may come in."* It pictures a victorious King entering His city. The question is asked and answered repeatedly: *"Who is this King of glory? The Lord strong and mighty, the Lord mighty in battle."* Psalm 24 may have been used during processions into Jerusalem, but it also points forward to Christ, the King of glory, who entered not just a city, but heaven itself.

Key Verse: (v.8)
"Who is this King of glory? The Lord strong and mighty, the Lord mighty in battle."

Application:

Psalm 24 reminds us to honour God as both Creator and King. If we desire to meet with Him, we must pursue purity and truth. But it also fills us with awe - our King is victorious, glorious, and strong. Make your heart a gate that welcomes Him in.

PSALM 25

Author: David

Theme: A prayer for guidance, forgiveness, and deliverance.

Summary:

Psalm 25 is a deeply personal prayer where David seeks God's help in the face of shame, sin, and enemies. *"In you, Lord my God, I put my trust."* This opening sets the tone for the entire Psalm: a humble, trusting heart turned toward God.

David asks that he would not be put to shame, and that his enemies would not triumph over him. He declares that hope in the Lord leads to honour, not disgrace. Then he prays, *"Show me your ways, Lord, teach me your paths."* He desires not just rescue, but righteousness. He wants to know God's will and walk in it. David appeals to God's mercy, asking that past sins would be forgiven: *"Do not remember the sins of my youth... according to your love remember me."*

He affirms that the Lord instructs sinners and guides the humble. All God's ways are *"loving and faithful"* to those who keep His covenant. David continues to seek guidance, forgiveness, and deliverance. He acknowledges his own affliction and loneliness and pleads for protection from his enemies.

The Psalm ends with an intercessory note: *"Deliver Israel, O God, from all their troubles."* Though personal, David's prayer includes his people, showing a shepherd's heart for the nation.

Key Verse: (v.4)

"Show me your ways, Lord, teach me your paths."

Application:

Psalm 25 encourages us to pray with humility and hope. We can ask God to guide us, forgive us, and defend us. He is faithful to those who seek Him sincerely. When overwhelmed by sin or opposition, lift your soul to the Lord - He will not fail you.

PSALM 26

Author: David

Theme: A plea for vindication based on a life of integrity.

Summary:
Psalm 26 is a personal appeal from David, who asks God to vindicate him because he has walked with integrity. *"I have trusted in the Lord and have not faltered,"* he declares. This isn't self-righteous boasting; it's a sincere affirmation of a heart committed to faithfulness, even under pressure.

David invites God to *"test me, Lord, and try me, examine my heart and my mind."* He welcomes divine scrutiny, confident that his loyalty to God is genuine. He avoids the deceitful and hypocritical and refuses to align himself with the wicked. *"I do not sit with the deceitful, nor do I associate with hypocrites."* Instead, he chooses the way of worship and righteousness. He washes his hands in innocence and proclaims God's praise, loving the house of the Lord where God's glory dwells. He desires not only to live rightly, but to delight in God's presence.

David pleads not to be swept away with sinners or bloodthirsty men, whose hands are full of evil. He sets himself apart from them, again not out of pride, but out of a desire to walk blamelessly before God. He concludes by expressing his commitment to continue on the right path: *"My feet stand on level ground; in the great congregation I will praise the Lord."*

Key Verse: (v.2)
"Test me, Lord, and try me, examine my heart and my mind."

Application:
Psalm 26 challenges us to live with integrity - not perfection, but a consistent, honest walk with God. It calls us to be people who love God's presence, avoid corruption, and welcome His refining gaze. Let your life be an open book before the Lord, shaped by truth and marked by worship.

PSALM 27

Author: David

Theme: Confidence in God's protection and presence.

Summary:

Psalm 27 is a bold declaration of faith in God's presence and power. *"The Lord is my light and my salvation – whom shall I fear?"* David opens with confidence, proclaiming that God is his refuge against every threat. Even when enemies advance, they will stumble and fall.

Though he faces real danger - armies encamping against him - David's heart is not shaken. His deepest desire is not military victory, but spiritual intimacy: *"One thing I ask from the Lord… that I may dwell in the house of the Lord all the days of my life."* He longs to gaze upon the beauty of the Lord and seek Him in His temple. David finds strength in worship. In God's presence, he is safe, with his head lifted above his enemies, he offers sacrifices with joy and sings praises to God.

Yet the Psalm also shifts in tone. David pleads, *"Do not hide your face from me… Do not reject me or forsake me."* He is honest about his fears and longing for reassurance. Even if abandoned by family, he declares, *"The Lord will receive me."* He asks for guidance: *"Teach me your way, Lord; lead me in a straight path."* Despite the threats around him, David waits on the Lord with patient hope. *"I remain confident of this: I will see the goodness of the Lord in the land of the living."*

Key Verse: (v.1)

"The Lord is my light and my salvation - whom shall I fear?"

Application:

This Psalm invites us to live from a place of worship-driven confidence. When fear rises, seek God's presence. When the path ahead is unclear, ask for His guidance. Like David, we can trust that God is our salvation - both now and forever.

PSALM 28

Author: David

Theme: A plea for mercy and a song of thanksgiving.

Summary:

Psalm 28 begins with urgency: *"To you, Lord, I call; you are my Rock, do not turn a deaf ear to me."* David fears the silence of God - *"If you remain silent, I will be like those who go down to the pit."* He longs not just for deliverance, but for a response that reassures him of God's presence.

David asks not to be dragged away with the wicked - those who speak peace while harbouring evil in their hearts. He calls on God to deal with them according to their deeds. This is not personal vengeance, but a cry for divine justice.

The Psalm then turns from petition to praise: *"Praise be to the Lord, for he has heard my cry for mercy."* David's tone shifts from desperation to relief. God has answered, and David now proclaims, *"The Lord is my strength and my shield; my heart trusts in him, and he helps me."* The one who began in fear ends in joy.

David rejoices not only for himself but also intercedes for his people: *"Save your people and bless your inheritance; be their shepherd and carry them forever."* This priestly ending shows David's heart as a leader who not only seeks God's help personally but longs for national blessing.

Key Verse: (v.7)

"The Lord is my strength and my shield; my heart trusts in him, and he helps me."

Application:

Psalm 28 reminds us that prayer can move us from fear to faith. Even when God feels silent, keep calling out. He is our Rock, our strength, and our shield. Trust in Him, and like David, you'll find joy in His faithful response - and confidence in His care for all His people.

PSALM 29

Author: David

Theme: The majestic voice of the Lord and His power.

Summary:
Psalm 29 is a majestic hymn celebrating the voice of the Lord. It opens with a call to worship: *"Ascribe to the Lord, you heavenly beings, ascribe to the Lord glory and strength."* All creation - and especially heavenly hosts - are summoned to honour the glory due His name.

David paints a vivid picture of God's voice. *"The voice of the Lord is over the waters… The voice of the Lord is powerful… The voice of the Lord breaks the cedars."* Each image builds in intensity, revealing God's voice as a force that shakes creation. Mountains leap, forests are stripped bare, deserts quake.

The imagery is not only dramatic but awe-inspiring. God's voice thunders over the seas, flashes with lightning, and causes entire landscapes to respond. Yet within that power lies purpose. The same voice that brings judgment also brings peace.

The Psalm concludes on a note of comfort and hope. *"The Lord sits enthroned over the flood; the Lord is enthroned as King forever."* He is not merely a distant force - He is a sovereign King who blesses His people with strength and peace.

Key Verse: (v.11)
"The Lord gives strength to his people; the Lord blesses his people with peace."

Application:
Psalm 29 reminds us that the power of God is not chaotic - it is ordered, majestic, and good. His voice brings change but also blessing.

Worship Him for His greatness and rest in His strength. In every storm, He remains enthroned.

PSALM 30

Author: David

Theme: Joy that follows sorrow.

Summary:

Psalm 30 is a Psalm of thanksgiving, written for the dedication of the temple, but rooted in David's personal experience of deliverance. *"I will exalt you, Lord, for you lifted me out of the depths."* David gives thanks for rescue from what seemed like certain defeat - or even death.

He acknowledges God's mercy: *"Lord my God, I called to you for help, and you healed me."* He had been at the brink - *"You, Lord, brought me up from the realm of the dead"* - but God intervened. In gratitude, David calls others to join him: *"Sing the praises of the Lord, you his faithful people."*

Then comes one of the most comforting verses in all of Scripture: *"Weeping may stay for the night, but rejoicing comes in the morning."* This line captures the rhythm of spiritual life - sorrow may be real, but it is never final.

David confesses his previous self-confidence: *"When I felt secure, I said, 'I will never be shaken.'"* But when God hid His face, he was dismayed. His strength came not from circumstances but from God's favour. He cried out for mercy, and God turned his mourning into dancing. *"You removed my sackcloth and clothed me with joy."* The Psalm closes with a vow to never stop praising the One who turned his cries into a song.

Key Verse: (v.5)

"Weeping may stay for the night, but rejoicing comes in the morning."

Application:

Psalm 30 encourages us to remember God's faithfulness in times of crisis. He is the One who lifts us up, heals us, and restores our joy. When sorrow feels overwhelming, hold on - joy is on the way. Praise is the final word for those who trust in Him.

PSALM 31

Author: David

Theme: Trusting God through fear, grief, and betrayal.

Summary:

Psalm 31 is a heartfelt prayer of trust in the midst of danger, distress, and betrayal. David begins with a familiar plea: *"In you, Lord, I have taken refuge."* He asks God to be his rock, fortress, and rescuer - foundational images of divine security. David affirms God's faithfulness: *"Into your hands I commit my spirit"* - a line Jesus would later speak on the cross. Despite being surrounded by enemies, David chooses to entrust his very life into God's hands. He knows that God is his deliverer.

The middle of the Psalm shifts into lament. David is in anguish. *"My eyes grow weak with sorrow, my soul and body with grief."* He feels forgotten and despised, even among his close companions. *"I am a broken vessel,"* he says. This is the language of someone who feels used up, cast aside, and overwhelmed.

And yet, even here, faith holds fast: *"But I trust in you, Lord; I say, 'You are my God.'"* David's enemies may scheme, but he believes his times are in God's hands. He calls on the Lord to let His face shine on him and to save him in His unfailing love.

The Psalm ends in praise and testimony. God heard his cry, showed him love, and did not hand him over to his enemies. David urges others to love the Lord and be strong: *"Be strong and take heart, all you who hope in the Lord."*

Key Verse: (v.14)

"But I trust in you, Lord; I say, 'You are my God.'"

Application:

Psalm 31 teaches us that even in moments of profound pain and fear, we can entrust ourselves to God. When others fail us and we feel crushed, His love remains unfailing. Commit your spirit into His hands - He is faithful to rescue and restore.

PSALM 32

Author: David

Theme: The joy of forgiveness and the freedom of confession.

Summary:

Psalm 32 celebrates the relief and joy that come from being forgiven. *"Blessed is the one whose transgressions are forgiven, whose sins are covered."* David reflects on the burden of unconfessed sin - how his bones wasted away and his strength was sapped. He lived under the weight of guilt until he finally acknowledged his sin to God.

"I said, 'I will confess my transgressions to the Lord.' And you forgave the guilt of my sin." That simple act of honest confession brought immediate and complete forgiveness. David then encourages everyone to turn to God in prayer while He may be found. The Lord becomes a hiding place and a refuge who protects and surrounds with songs of deliverance. God responds within the Psalm, promising to instruct and guide: *"I will counsel you with my loving eye on you."* We are warned not to be like stubborn animals that must be controlled by bit and bridle. God's guidance is personal and relational, not forced.

David contrasts the many woes of the wicked with the security of those who trust in the Lord. The Psalm ends with a call to joy: *"Rejoice in the Lord and be glad, you righteous; sing, all you who are upright in heart!"*

Key Verse: (v.1)

"Blessed is the one whose transgressions are forgiven, whose sins are covered."

Application:

Psalm 32 reminds us that hiding sin leads to misery, but confessing it brings peace. God doesn't desire our perfection - He desires our honesty. When we admit our failure, He offers forgiveness, protection, and joyful freedom. Don't delay - come to Him with a sincere heart.

PSALM 33

Author: Anonymous

Theme: Praising God for His power, righteousness, and faithful love.

Summary:

Psalm 33 is a joyful call to praise the Lord with music, song, and shouts of joy. *"Sing joyfully to the Lord, you righteous; it is fitting for the upright to praise him."* God is worthy of worship because His Word is right, His works are faithful, and His love fills the earth.

The Psalm celebrates God's creative power: *"By the word of the Lord the heavens were made, their starry host by the breath of his mouth."* God spoke - and the universe came into being. The Lord's plans stand firm forever.

Nations may rise and fall, but His purposes prevail. *"Blessed is the nation whose God is the Lord,"* the Psalm declares - reminding Israel, and us, that true security is found not in armies or wealth, but in the fear of the Lord.

God watches over all humanity. He sees every heart and considers every deed. Kings are not saved by great armies, nor warriors by their strength. *"A horse is a vain hope for deliverance"* - victory comes from God alone. The Psalm ends with a prayer of trust: *"We wait in hope for the Lord; he is our help and our shield."* His unfailing love rests on those who hope in Him.

Key Verse: (v.11)

"But the plans of the Lord stand firm forever, the purposes of his heart through all generations."

Application:

Psalm 33 calls us to place our confidence in God, not in human power. God is Creator, Sustainer, and Redeemer. Praise Him for His greatness and always rest in His plans. No matter what happens in the world around us, His Word never fails, and His love never ends.

PSALM 34

Author: David

Theme: God delivers and blesses those who fear Him.

Summary:

Psalm 34 is a song of praise born from personal experience. After being rescued from a dangerous situation, David declares, *"I will extol the Lord at all times; his praise will always be on my lips."* He invites others to join him in glorifying God: *"Let us exalt his name together."*

David testifies that when he sought the Lord, He answered. *"Those who look to him are radiant... this poor man called, and the Lord heard him."* God doesn't just hear prayers - He sends deliverance. *"The angel of the Lord encamps around those who fear him, and he delivers them."* The Psalm includes one of its most memorable invitations: *"Taste and see that the Lord is good."* David urges his readers to take refuge in God and learn the fear of the Lord. fear of the Lord leads to a life of blessing - speaking truth, turning from evil, doing good, and seeking peace. *"The eyes of the Lord are on the righteous... but the face of the Lord is against those who do evil."*

David doesn't deny the reality of suffering. *"The righteous person may have many troubles,"* he writes, *"but the Lord delivers him from them all."* Even when bones are broken, God protects. The Psalm ends with a promise: the Lord redeems His servants, and none who take refuge in Him will be condemned.

Key Verse: (v.8)

"Taste and see that the Lord is good; blessed is the one who takes refuge in him."

Application:

Psalm 34 encourages us to trust God not just in theory, but through lived experience. Cry out, seek Him, and take refuge in His goodness. Though troubles may come, God will hear and deliver you. He is near to the broken-hearted and faithful to all who trust in Him.

PSALM 35

Author: David

Theme: A cry for justice in the face of false accusation.

Summary:

Psalm 35 is an intense and personal appeal from David for God's intervention. He begins with a bold cry: *"Contend, Lord, with those who contend with me; fight against those who fight against me."* This is courtroom language - David is asking God to take up his case, to be his divine defender against unjust enemies.

He calls on God to rise as a warrior on his behalf: *"Take up shield and armour; arise and come to my aid."* David's enemies are not merely foreign invader- they are close companions who have turned against him. *"They repay me evil for good and leave me like one bereaved."* The injustice is not just painful - it feels cruel.

He pleads with God: *"How long, Lord, will you look on? Rescue me from their ravages."* David longs for vindication - not to glorify himself, but so that he can publicly praise the Lord. *"I will give you thanks in the great assembly; among the throngs I will praise you."*

He asks that his enemies would not triumph or gloat over him. He knows they have no cause for their attacks and that they speak falsely and maliciously. Yet despite his anguish, David entrusts the situation to God and ends with hope: *"My tongue will proclaim your righteousness, your praises all day long."*

Key Verse: (v.1)

"Contend, Lord, with those who contend with me; fight against those who fight against me."

Application:

Psalm 35 teaches us to bring every injustice to the Lord. When you're slandered, betrayed, or falsely accused, you don't need to seek revenge. God is your advocate. He sees the truth, hears your cry, and will act in His time. Trust in His righteousness - and let your response be praise.

PSALM 36

Author: David

Theme: The contrast between human wickedness
and God's unfailing love

Summary:

Psalm 36 begins with a sobering observation: *"I have a message from God in my heart concerning the sinfulness of the wicked."* David describes how the wicked live without fear of God. They flatter themselves too much to recognize or hate their sin.

But then the Psalm turns dramatically from human depravity to divine majesty. David declares, *"Your love, Lord, reaches to the heavens, your faithfulness to the skies."* God's righteousness is like the highest mountains, His justice like the great deep. In contrast to human sin, God's character is vast, pure, and dependable.

David celebrates God's kindness: *"How priceless is your unfailing love, O God! People take refuge in the shadow of your wings."* God provides not only shelter but abundance. His people feast on the abundance of His house and drink from His river of delights. *"For with you is the fountain of life; in your light we see light."*

The Psalm concludes with a prayer: David asks that God's love continue for those who know Him and that the proud and wicked would not overpower him. *"See how the evildoers lie fallen - thrown down, not able to rise!"*

Key Verse: (v.7)

"How priceless is your unfailing love, O God! People take refuge in the shadow of your wings."

Application:

Psalm 36 reminds us that while human evil is real and pervasive, it is no match for the vastness of God's love and justice. Don't let the wickedness of the world steal your hope. Take refuge in God's presence, delight in His abundance, and live in the light of His truth.

PSALM 37

Author: David

Theme: Trusting in God's justice.

Summary:

Psalm 37 is a wisdom Psalm filled with practical guidance for righteous living in the face of injustice. David begins with a command: *"Do not fret because of those who are evil or be envious of those who do wrong."* Though the wicked may appear to thrive, they are like grass - soon withered and gone. David urges the reader to trust in the Lord and do good. *"Take delight in the Lord, and he will give you the desires of your heart."* This isn't a promise of worldly gain but an assurance that God satisfies those who find their joy in Him. *"Commit your way to the Lord… and he will make your righteous reward shine like the dawn."*

Throughout the Psalm, David contrasts the fate of the wicked and the righteous. The wicked plot and prosper temporarily, but their weapons will turn against them. *"Better the little that the righteous have than the wealth of many wicked."* David speaks from experience: *"I was young and now I am old, yet I have never seen the righteous forsaken."* He assures us that the Lord loves justice and will not abandon His faithful ones.

The Psalm ends with a reaffirmation of God's loving care. *"The salvation of the righteous comes from the Lord; he is their stronghold in time of trouble."* The Lord will help and deliver those who take refuge in Him.

Key Verse: (v.1)

"Do not fret because of those who are evil or be envious of those who do wrong."

Application:

Psalm 37 encourages patience and faith when life feels unfair. Don't let temporary injustice rob you of peace. Delight in God, do good, and trust Him to bring justice. The wicked may seem secure, but only those who trust in the Lord will endure.

PSALM 38

Author: David

Theme: A prayer of repentance and physical-spiritual anguish.

Summary:
Psalm 38 is a powerful expression of confession and suffering. David begins with a plea: *"Lord, do not rebuke me in your anger or discipline me in your wrath."* He feels the weight of God's hand - his body is afflicted, his bones ache, and his guilt overwhelms.

He writes, *"My guilt has overwhelmed me like a burden too heavy to bear."* His wounds fester, his strength fails, and he is utterly crushed. This Psalm vividly describes the toll that sin can take - not just spiritually, but emotionally and physically. David is isolated and despairing. *"I am bowed down and brought very low."*

His friends and companions stand at a distance. His enemies are active, laying traps and seeking his downfall. Yet he does not respond with defence or argument. Instead, he turns inward, acknowledging his brokenness and waiting for the Lord. *"I wait for you, O Lord; you will answer, Lord my God."*

David confesses his iniquity and mourns over his sin. He sees his suffering as just, but he still pleads for help and deliverance. *"Lord, do not forsake me; do not be far from me, my God. Come quickly to help me, my Lord and my Saviour."*

Key Verse: (v.4)
"My guilt has overwhelmed me like a burden too heavy to bear."

Application:
Psalm 38 reminds us that it's okay to bring the full weight of our sin and sorrow to God. There is no need to hide. When guilt crushes you and relationships break down, turn to the Lord with honesty and humility. He is both just and merciful - and He will not turn away a contrite heart.

PSALM 39

Author: David

Theme: The brevity of life and the hope found in God

Summary:

Psalm 39 begins with self-restraint. David is troubled but chooses not to speak, lest he sin with his tongue. Yet the fire inside him burns, and he finally speaks - not to people, but to God. *"Show me, Lord, my life's end and the number of my days; let me know how fleeting my life is."*

David reflects on the shortness of life. *"You have made my days a mere handbreadth."* Human existence is a breath, a shadow, quickly passing. People rush around in vain, heaping up wealth, not knowing who will benefit from it.

These sobering thoughts lead him to a single conclusion: *"But now, Lord, what do I look for? My hope is in you."*

He asks God to deliver him from his transgressions and not let him be the scorn of fools. He feels the sting of divine discipline but does not accuse God. Rather, he pleads for mercy: *"Look away from me, that I may enjoy life again before I depart and am no more."*

This Psalm is a reflection on mortality, repentance, and the deep yearning for meaning that only God can satisfy.

Key Verse: (v.7)

"But now, Lord, what do I look for? My hope is in you."

Application:

Psalm 39 urges us to live with eternal perspective. Life is short, and our only lasting hope is in God. Don't waste your days chasing temporary things.

Instead, confess your sin, look to God for meaning, and fix your eyes on eternity.

PSALM 40

Author: David

Theme: A song of deliverance, trust, and renewed need

Summary:

Psalm 40 opens with praise for answered prayer. *"I waited patiently for the Lord; he turned to me and heard my cry."* God lifted David out of the pit, set his feet on a rock, and gave him a new song of praise. Many will see and fear the Lord because of what He has done.

David declares the joy of trusting in God rather than relying on the proud or following lies. He celebrates God's wonderful deeds and thoughts toward His people — too many to declare. He then speaks of wholehearted devotion: *"Sacrifice and offering you did not desire... I desire to do your will, my God."*

This Psalm is also messianic, pointing forward to Jesus, who fulfilled God's will perfectly. David proclaims righteousness in the great assembly and does not hide the truth about God's love and faithfulness.

But then the tone shifts. David once again faces trouble. *"My sins have overtaken me, and I cannot see."* He asks for mercy, for rescue, for protection from those who seek to destroy him. Still, he ends with hope: *"May all who seek you rejoice and be glad in you... You are my help and my deliverer; you are my God, do not delay."*

Key Verse: (v.2)

"He lifted me out of the slimy pit... he set my feet on a rock and gave me a firm place to stand."

Application:

Psalm 40 reminds us that God's past faithfulness gives us confidence for today's troubles. When you're rescued, testify. When you are surrounded again, cry out. He is always your deliverer. Wait patiently, walk obediently, and trust His timing.

PSALM 41

Author: David

Theme: God's mercy and protection.

Summary:

Psalm 41 opens with a blessing for those who care for the weak: *"Blessed are those who have regard for the weak; the Lord delivers them in times of trouble."* David affirms that God will protect and sustain the compassionate.

David then turns to his personal situation. He is unwell and surrounded by enemies. *"Have mercy on me, Lord; heal me, for I have sinned against you."* He recognizes his own failings while trusting in God's grace. Meanwhile, adversaries whisper about his ruin and wait for him to die. Their words are cruel, and even close friends have turned against him. *"Even my close friend, someone I trusted, one who shared my bread, has turned against me."*

David pleads for God to raise him up so that justice may be done. His hope is not in vengeance, but in being vindicated by God's mercy. *"But may you have mercy on me, Lord; raise me up, that I may repay them."* He knows that God delights in him and upholds him because of his integrity. The Psalm ends with a really joyful affirmation: *"Praise be to the Lord, the God of Israel, from everlasting to everlasting. Amen and Amen."* This doxology also concludes Book I of the Psalms, marking a turning point in the collection.

Key Verse: (v.1)

"Blessed are those who have regard for the weak; the Lord delivers them in times of trouble."

Application:

Psalm 41 reminds us that God always honours compassion and faithfulness. When you care for the weak, you reflect the heart of God - and He promises to care for you. When you are betrayed or physically weakened, turn to God, who alone heals, defends, and restores. Like David, you can praise Him in the midst of your trouble, knowing that He is always faithful.

PSALM 42

Author: Sons of Korah

Theme: Deep longing for God.

Summary:

Psalm 42 begins with an image of desperate thirst: *"As the deer pants for streams of water, so my soul pants for you, my God."* This is not a gentle yearning - it is a cry from the depths of spiritual dryness and longing. The Psalmist is feeling abandoned and disheartened, mocked by others who ask, *"Where is your God?"*

He remembers better days - when he went with the throng to the house of God, shouting with joy and thanksgiving. But now he feels far from that joy, and his soul is downcast within him. Still, he does not give in to despair. He begins to speak to his own soul: *"Why, my soul, are you downcast? Why so disturbed within me? Put your hope in God, for I will yet praise him, my Savior and my God."*

This refrain becomes the anchor of the Psalm. Though he feels forgotten as deep calls to deep and waves of sorrow overwhelm him, he clings to hope. He says, *"By day the Lord directs his love, at night his song is with me."* These words do not deny his pain - they push through it with determined faith. The Psalmist is honest: he feels oppressed, forgotten, and taunted.

The Psalm ends as it began: with honest lament and a renewed commitment to hope. *"For I will yet praise him."*

Key Verse: (v.5)

"Why, my soul, are you downcast? Why so disturbed within me? Put your hope in God."

Application:

Psalm 42 teaches us how to walk through spiritual depression with faith. When you feel abandoned, keep talking to God - and to yourself. Remind your soul of His love and truth. Keep hoping. Keep praising. Even when you can't feel God's presence, you can choose to trust in His unfailing love.

PSALM 43

Author: Anonymous

Theme: A longing for restoration and return to joyful worship.

Summary:

Psalm 43 continues the lament of Psalm 42, with the same refrain and same emotional tone. The Psalmist pleads for vindication: *"Vindicate me, my God, and plead my cause against an unfaithful nation."* He is surrounded by deceit and injustice and longs for God to intervene. The sense of abandonment continues: *"You are God my stronghold. Why have you rejected me?"*

The Psalmist does not stay in despair. He asks God to send out His light and truth to guide him back to His presence. *"Send me your light and your faithful care, let them lead me; let them bring me to your holy mountain."* His longing is not just for relief, but for restored worship.

He envisions returning to the altar of God, where he will praise with joy and music. *"Then I will go to the altar of God, to God, my joy and my delight."* Worship is not a formality - it is a reunion with the One who brings true gladness.

The refrain returns a final time: *"Why, my soul, are you downcast? Put your hope in God, for I will yet praise him."* This internal dialogue anchors his heart when his surroundings remain hostile.

Key Verse: (v.3)

"Send me your light and your faithful care, let them lead me."

Application:

Psalm 43 encourages us to seek God's guidance when we feel lost. In the midst of injustice, sorrow, or spiritual distance, ask for His light and truth. He will lead you back to joy and worship. Keep speaking truth to your soul - God has not rejected you. He will restore you again.

PSALM 44

Author: Sons of Korah

Theme: Remembering God's faithfulness.

Summary:

Psalm 44 opens with a confident declaration of God's past faithfulness. *"We have heard it with our ears, O God, our ancestors have told us what you did in their days."* The Psalmist remembers how God gave Israel victory - not by their own sword or their strength, but by His power and favour.

These recollections then inspire present trust. *"You are my King and my God,"* he says, rejoicing that it is through God they push back their enemies. *"I put no trust in my bow, my sword does not bring me victory."*

But suddenly, the tone changes. Despite their faith, the people now suffer defeat and disgrace. *"You have rejected and humbled us… You made us retreat before the enemy."* They are scattered among the nations, sold for nothing, and made a reproach and ridicule to their neighbours. This suffering seems undeserved. *"All this came upon us, though we had not forgotten you… our hearts had not turned back."*

The Psalmist then cries out with raw honesty: *"Awake, Lord! Why do you sleep? Rouse yourself! Do not reject us forever."* He pleads with God to see their suffering and to act, not for their merit, but because of His unfailing love. The final verse is a passionate appeal: *"Rise up and help us; rescue us because of your unfailing love."*

Key Verse: (v.26)

"Rise up and help us; rescue us because of your unfailing love."

Application:

Psalm 44 reminds us that even the faithful can experience suffering that feels unjust. When God seems silent, we can still call on Him honestly. He welcomes lament that clings to His love. Keep praying, keep remembering, and trust that the God of your ancestors will rise again.

PSALM 45

Author: Sons of Korah

Theme: A royal wedding song celebrating the Messiah-King.

Summary:

Psalm 45 is a royal Psalm, originally composed as a wedding song for the king of Israel. However, its language and tone quickly elevate it beyond any earthly monarch. The Psalmist begins with heartfelt enthusiasm: *"My heart is stirred by a noble theme as I recite my verses for the king."* This sets the tone for a song that honours a majestic figure - both king and bridegroom.

The king is praised for his beauty, strength, truth, humility, and righteousness. *"You are the most excellent of men and your lips have been anointed with grace.* In verses 6 and 7, the language shifts in a striking way: *"Your throne, O God, will last for ever and ever... therefore God, your God, has set you above your companions."* These verses are later quoted in Hebrews 1:8–9, referring to Christ.

The bride is then introduced - she is urged to forget her former home and embrace her new royal identity. *"The king is enthralled by your beauty; honour him, for he is your lord."* The Psalm ends with a blessing over the royal union. What began as a celebration of a human king's wedding becomes a prophetic song of the eternal reign of Christ.

Key Verse: (v.6)
"Your throne, O God, will last for ever and ever; a sceptre of justice will be the sceptre of your kingdom."

Application:

Psalm 45 invites us to gaze upon our King - Jesus Christ - with adoration and awe. He is perfect in righteousness, majestic in power, and full of grace. As His bride, we are called to honour Him, submit to His leadership, and rejoice in His love. Let your heart be stirred by this noble theme and offer your life in praise to the King who reigns forever.

PSALM 46

Author: Sons of Korah

Theme: God is our refuge in times of chaos and conflict.

Summary:

Psalm 46 begins with unshakable confidence: *"God is our refuge and strength, an ever-present help in trouble."* This opening verse sets the tone for the entire Psalm - a declaration that even in the worst circumstances, God remains constant and faithful.

"Therefore we will not fear, though the earth give way and the mountains fall into the heart of the sea." The imagery is dramatic: earthquakes, floods, and trembling nations. Yet through it all, the Psalmist insists, there is no need to fear because God is with us.

The Psalm speaks of a river whose streams make glad the city of God - a picture of spiritual refreshment and divine presence. *"God is within her, she will not fall; God will help her at break of day."* Even when kingdoms fall and the earth melts, the Lord Almighty remains unshaken. A powerful refrain runs through the Psalm: *"The Lord Almighty is with us; the God of Jacob is our fortress."* This truth anchors the people of God, no matter the chaos around them.

The final section calls for stillness: He says, *"Be still, and know that I am God."* In a world of noise, God's voice calls us to rest in His sovereignty. He will be exalted among the nations and in all the earth and the miracle is we can know this mighty God!

Key Verse: (v.10)
"Be still and know that I am God."

Application:

Psalm 46 is a reminder that God is greater than any storm, disaster, or threat. When life feels unstable, find refuge in Him. He is your fortress, always present and unshaken. Be still - not because the world is calm, but because your God is in control.

PSALM 47

Author: Sons of Korah

Theme: Exalting God as King over all the earth.

Summary:

Psalm 47 is a jubilant call to worship the sovereign King. *"Clap your hands, all you nations; shout to God with cries of joy."* It's not a quiet or reserved praise - it's a loud, universal celebration of God's rule. He is not just Israel's God; He is *"the great King over all the earth."*

The Psalm praises God's power: *"He subdued nations under us, peoples under our feet."* It reflects on how God gave the land to His people, fulfilling His covenant promises. But more than just a national anthem, this Psalm proclaims a cosmic truth - God reigns above all.

"God has ascended amid shouts of joy, the Lord amid the sounding of trumpets." This verse points forward to Christ's ascension and victory. The Psalm invites us to sing praises repeatedly: *"Sing praises to God, sing praises!"*

The final verses highlight God's universal dominion: *"God reigns over the nations; God is seated on his holy throne."* Earthly rulers and kings are ultimately under His authority. He is exalted above all.

This Psalm likely accompanied processions into the temple or commemorated royal events, but its language also expands to include all peoples and all time.

Key Verse: (v.8)

"God reigns over the nations; God is seated on his holy throne."

Application:

Psalm 47 invites us to celebrate God's universal reign with joy and awe. No matter who sits on earthly thrones, God reigns supreme. Praise Him not just for what He has done for you, but because He is King over all. Lift your voice - He is worthy.

PSALM 48

Author: Sons of Korah

Theme: The glory and security of God's presence.

Summary:

Psalm 48 is a song celebrating the city of God – Jerusalem - not because of its architecture, but because God is present there. *"Great is the Lord, and most worthy of praise, in the city of our God."* It speaks of Mount Zion, beautiful in elevation, the joy of the whole earth.

God's presence in the city makes it unshakable. *"God is in her citadels; he has shown himself to be her fortress."* When kings joined forces to attack, they saw her and fled in terror. This is not a testament to human strength, but to divine protection.

The Psalm recounts how people ponder God's unfailing love within His temple and celebrate His name throughout the earth. *"Like your name, O God, your praise reaches to the ends of the earth."* God's right hand is filled with righteousness, and His judgments bring joy to His people. Then comes a personal exhortation: *"Walk about Zion... count her towers... consider well her ramparts."* The people are invited to reflect on the security and greatness of God's dwelling, so they may tell future generations.

The Psalm closes with a beautiful affirmation: *"For this God is our God for ever and ever; he will be our guide even to the end."* God is not just a distant deity - He is their eternal guide.

Key Verse: (v.14)
"For this God is our God for ever and ever; he will be our guide even to the end."

Application:

Psalm 48 reminds us that our security is found in God's presence, not in human strength. Celebrate the greatness of the Lord and the joy of belonging to Him. He is our guide, not just in this life but forever. Walk confidently - He dwells among His people.

PSALM 49

Author: Sons of Korah

Theme: The futility of wealth and the certainty of death.

Summary:
Psalm 49 is a wisdom Psalm, calling people of every status to listen: *"Hear this, all you peoples; listen, all who live in this world."* The subject is universal - wealth, mortality, and the false security found in riches. *"Why should I fear when evil days come… when men trust in their wealth?"*

The Psalmist warns that no one can redeem another or give God a ransom for them. *"The ransom for a life is costly, no payment is ever enough."* All people - rich or poor - face the same end: death. The wise and foolish alike perish, leaving all their wealth behind.

People name lands after themselves and build enduring homes, but they cannot escape the grave. *"People, despite their wealth, do not endure; they are like the beasts that perish."* Riches may provide comfort in life, but they offer no security in death. Yet the Psalmist declares hope: *"But God will redeem me from the realm of the dead; he will surely take me to himself."* This foreshadows the hope of resurrection and eternal life. The righteous need not fear when the wicked grow rich.

The Psalm closes with a warning: *"People who have wealth but lack understanding are like the beasts that perish."* Wisdom and trust in God are of far greater value than riches.

Key Verse: (v.15)
"But God will redeem me from the realm of the dead; he will surely take me to himself."

Application:
Psalm 49 teaches us to measure life by eternal values, not earthly wealth. Riches cannot save you. Only God can redeem your soul. Place your trust in Him, not in what you possess. Live wisely and walk humbly with the One who holds eternity.

PSALM 50

Author: Asaph

Theme: True worship, divine justice, and the heart God desires.

Summary:

Psalm 50 opens with a dramatic and awe-inspiring vision of God. *"The Mighty One, God, the Lord, speaks and summons the earth from the rising of the sun to where it sets."* God is not silent. From Zion, His perfect dwelling place, He shines forth in radiant glory. Asaph paints a picture of divine judgment but the judgment is not directed at the nations - it begins with His covenant people. *"Gather to me this consecrated people, who made a covenant with me by sacrifice."* He challenges the heart behind their worship. *"I have no need of a bull from your stall or of goats from your pens."*

Instead, what He desires is thankfulness and trust: *"Sacrifice thank offerings to God, fulfill your vows to the Most High, and call on me in the day of trouble; I will deliver you, and you will honour me."*

The second half of the Psalm is directed toward the wicked among His people - those who recite His statutes but reject His discipline. *"You hate my instruction and cast my words behind you."* They join with thieves, commit adultery, and speak slander against their own family.

The Psalm ends with a stark choice. *"Consider this, you who forget God, or I will tear you to pieces, with no one to rescue you."* But it also offers hope: *"Those who sacrifice thank offerings honour me, and to the blameless I will show my salvation."*

Key Verse: (v.14)

"Sacrifice thank offerings to God, fulfill your vows to the Most High."

Application:

Psalm 50 reminds us that God desires heartfelt worship, not hollow ritual. He looks for thankfulness, trust, and obedience. Examine your worship - does it flow from a grateful heart or a routine habit? True faith responds to God's grace with reverence, gratitude, and integrity.

PSALM 51

Author: David

Theme: A heartfelt plea for mercy and cleansing after sin.

Summary:

Psalm 51 is one of the most well-known penitential Psalms, written by David after the prophet Nathan confronted him about his sin with Bathsheba. It is a powerful confession that shows the depth of true repentance. David begins with an appeal to God's mercy: *"Have mercy on me, O God, according to your unfailing love; according to your great compassion blot out my transgressions."*

David uses several strong terms for sin: transgressions, iniquity, and sin. He knows that his wrongdoing is ultimately against God: *"Against you, you only, have I sinned and done what is evil in your sight."* He is not asking for a mere pardon; he longs to be changed from within. *"Create in me a pure heart, O God, and renew a steadfast spirit within me."* David recognizes that God desires truth in the inner being and a broken, contrite heart. External sacrifices are not what God truly seeks; He wants inward sincerity and humility. *"My sacrifice, O God, is a broken spirit; a broken and contrite heart you, God, will not despise."*

Even as he prays for personal cleansing, David also expresses concern for the well-being of God's people, indicating that true repentance leads to renewed concern for the whole community.

Key Verse: (v.10)
"Create in me a pure heart, O God, and renew a steadfast spirit within me."

Application:

Psalm 51 teaches us that genuine repentance involves more than regret. It is an honest acknowledgment of sin, a plea for mercy, and a desire for transformation. God does not despise a broken and contrite heart. When we fail, we can come to Him - not hiding but hoping in His compassion. Through Christ, our sin can be washed away, and we can be made new.

PSALM 52

Author: David

Theme: God will bring down the wicked
and uphold the righteous.

Summary:

Psalm 52 is a rebuke of a specific kind of evil person - one who uses deceit, power, and words to destroy. David begins by confronting the arrogance of the wicked: *"Why do you boast of evil, you mighty hero, why do you boast all day long, you who are a disgrace in the eyes of God?"* This mighty man trusts in destructive words and lies rather than truth. His tongue is likened to a sharpened razor, cutting and cruel. Yet God is not indifferent. The wicked man may flourish for a while, but God will uproot him forever. *"Surely God will bring you down to everlasting ruin."*

The Psalm then takes a sharp turn from judgment to hope. David contrasts the wicked man with himself: *"But I am like an olive tree flourishing in the house of God."* While the evildoer relied on his wealth and manipulation, David trusts in God's unfailing love. His roots are deep and his strength enduring - not because of his circumstances, but because of where he stands.

The final verses turn toward worship and patience: *"I will praise you forever for what you have done."* David will wait in hope for God's name, which is good and trustworthy.

Key Verse: (v.8)
*"But I am like an olive tree flourishing in the house of God;
I trust in God's unfailing love for ever and ever."*

Application:

Psalm 52 reminds us that evil may look powerful, but it is ultimately temporary. Do not be envious or fearful of those who seem to prosper through deceit or cruelty. Instead, choose the way of rooted trust in God. Like David, plant yourself in God's presence, and let your life be a testimony to His faithfulness. In the end, it is not the cunning but the faithful who will flourish.

PSALM 53

Author: David

Theme: The foolishness of denying God.

Summary:

Psalm 53 is a sobering reflection on human depravity. It begins with a stark declaration: *"The fool says in his heart, 'There is no God.'"* This is not merely an intellectual statement - it is a moral and spiritual rebellion. The fool in biblical terms is one who lives as though God does not exist, ignoring His authority and denying His truth. David observes that such denial leads to corruption: *"They are corrupt, and their ways are vile; there is no one who does good."* God looks down from heaven to see if anyone is wise, if anyone seeks Him. The result is disheartening: *"Everyone has turned away, all have become corrupt."* This Psalm echoes themes from Psalm 14 and is quoted by Paul in Romans 3 to describe the universal need for salvation.

But David assures us that God is not blind to this injustice. *"God will scatter the bones of those who attacked you; you put them to shame, for God despised them."* Their apparent strength will be shattered by divine judgment. The Psalm ends with hope: *"Oh, that salvation for Israel would come out of Zion!"* David anticipates a future redemption when God restores His people. When that happens, *"Jacob will rejoice and Israel will be glad."*

Key Verse: (v.1)

"The fool says in his heart, 'There is no God.' They are corrupt, and their ways are vile; there is no one who does good."

Application:

Psalm 53 is a warning against living as though God does not matter. Foolishness is not a lack of intelligence - it's a refusal to acknowledge God's presence and authority. Examine your heart: are you seeking God or ignoring Him? In a world that often mocks faith, let your life proclaim the reality of God through righteousness and trust. His salvation is sure, and those who hope in Him will rejoice.

PSALM 54

Author: David

Theme: Calling on God for deliverance in the face of betrayal.

Summary:

Psalm 54 is a short but passionate plea for help. David wrote it when the Ziphites betrayed him to Saul, revealing his location while he was fleeing for his life. He opens with a cry for rescue: *"Save me, O God, by your name; vindicate me by your might."* David knows where to turn when betrayal strikes - he appeals to God's character and power.

He acknowledges the threat: *"Arrogant foes are attacking me; ruthless people are trying to kill me - people without regard for God."* These are not mere enemies; they are godless opponents who act without conscience. Yet David does not collapse in fear. He immediately affirms, *"Surely God is my help; the Lord is the one who sustains me."*

He trusts that God will deal justly with his enemies: *"Let evil recoil on those who slander me; in your faithfulness destroy them."* David is confident that God sees and will act.

As the Psalm concludes, David shifts to thanksgiving. "I will sacrifice a freewill offering to you; I will praise your name, Lord, for it is good." He anticipates victory and expresses faith before the deliverance even comes. "You have delivered me from all my troubles, and my eyes have looked in triumph on my foes."

Key Verse: (v.4)

"Surely God is my help; the Lord is the one who sustains me."

Application:

Psalm 54 speaks to anyone who has felt betrayed or under threat. In moments of danger or abandonment, turn to God. He is your helper and sustainer. You don't need to retaliate - leave justice in His hands. Praise Him not only after the victory, but even in anticipation of it. God is faithful to those who trust Him.

PSALM 55

Author: David

Theme: The pain of betrayal and the peace
of casting burdens on God.

Summary:

Psalm 55 is a deeply emotional lament, expressing the anguish of betrayal by a close companion. David begins with desperation: *"Listen to my prayer, O God, do not ignore my plea."* He is overwhelmed, his thoughts in turmoil, and his heart in anguish. The fear is so intense he longs to escape: *"Oh, that I had the wings of a dove! I would fly away and be at rest."* He describes violence and strife in the city and a betrayal that cuts deeply: *"If an enemy were insulting me, I could endure it… but it is you, a man like myself, my companion, my close friend."* This betrayal wounds more because it came from someone who once worshipped alongside him.

David appeals to God to bring justice to those who spread destruction. *"Let death take my enemies by surprise; let them go down alive to the realm of the dead."* But in contrast to this judgment, David models a better path: *"As for me, I call to God, and the Lord saves me."* He prays evening, morning, and noon, confident that God hears his voice. The Psalm climaxes with an invitation that has comforted believers for generations: *"Cast your cares on the Lord and he will sustain you; he will never let the righteous be shaken."* God deals with the deceitful, but the righteous rest in His care.

Key Verse: (v.22)

"Cast your cares on the Lord and he will sustain you; he will never let the righteous be shaken."

Application:

Psalm 55 reminds us that betrayal is one of the most painful wounds, but God is a faithful refuge. When others fail you - even those closest to you - bring your burdens to the Lord. He is strong enough to carry them and gentle enough to care. Keep praying, even when peace feels far away. He will sustain you.

PSALM 56

Author: David

Theme: Trusting God through fear.

Summary:

Psalm 56 was written when David was seized by the Philistines in Gath. Despite being in enemy territory and under immense pressure, David's response is one of faith: *"Be merciful to me, my God, for my enemies are in hot pursuit; all day long they press their attack."* He does not deny the fear - but he knows where to take it. *"When I am afraid, I put my trust in you."*

This simple yet profound declaration appears twice in the Psalm. It is not the absence of fear that defines David's faith, but his choice to trust God amid fear. His enemies twist his words, plot against him, and lurk to take his life. Yet David holds firm: *"In God I trust and am not afraid. What can mere mortals do to me?"* He knows God sees his suffering: *"Record my misery; list my tears on your scroll - are they not in your record?"* This tender image reminds us that our pain is not forgotten. God treasures every tear. David's confidence grows as he declares that his enemies will turn back *"when I call for help."*

The Psalm closes with thanksgiving: *"I am under vows to you, my God; I will present my thank offerings to you."* David gives thanks in anticipation, not just for past deliverance but for future faithfulness.

Key Verse: (v.3)

"When I am afraid, I put my trust in you."

Application:

Psalm 56 is a lifeline for those struggling with fear or opposition. Faith is not the absence of fear - it's trusting God through it. God knows your pain and hears your cries. Like David, you can say, *"What can mere mortals do to me?"* because your life is in God's hands. Bring your tears to Him, and trust that He will act.

PSALM 57

Author: David

Theme: Praise in the midst of peril.

Summary:

Psalm 57 was written by David when he fled from Saul and hid in a cave. It is a beautiful expression of confidence in God's protection. He opens with a prayer: *"Have mercy on me, my God, have mercy on me, for in you I take refuge."* David describes sheltering *"in the shadow of your wings until the disaster has passed."* This is the language of trust under pressure.

Though surrounded by enemies, David still affirms God's sovereignty. *"I cry out to God Most High, to God, who vindicates me."* He believes that God will send help from heaven and save him, even as he lies *"amid ravenous beasts."* His enemies are fierce and deceptive, but David's heart remains steadfast. Twice he declares, *"Be exalted, O God, above the heavens; let your glory be over all the earth."* Even in hiding, he worships. His focus is not on his danger, but on God's glory. David says, *"My heart, O God, is steadfast... I will sing and make music."*

The Psalm ends with confident praise. David sees the dawn as a moment to awaken worship: *"I will awaken the dawn."* He wants not only to survive but to lift God's name among the nations.

Key Verse: (v.7)

"My heart, O God, is steadfast, my heart is steadfast; I will sing and make music."

Application:

Psalm 57 reminds us that worship is not just for peaceful moments. It's a weapon in times of trial. When you feel like you're hiding in a cave - let your heart remain steadfast.

Praise God not for the absence of trials, but for His presence in them. He is your refuge, and His glory will rise above your circumstances.

PSALM 58

Author: David

Theme: God will judge corruption and reward righteousness.

Summary:

Psalm 58 is a bold denunciation of unjust leaders. David opens with a piercing question: *"Do you rulers indeed speak justly? Do you judge people with equity?"* The implied answer is no. These leaders devise injustice in their hearts and distribute violence with their hands. Their corruption is not accidental - it is deliberate.

He describes them as *"wicked from birth,"* likening them to venomous snakes who refuse to listen. David calls on God to act with striking imagery: *"Break the teeth in their mouths, O God."* David is not content to just let wickedness rule unchecked. He uses vivid metaphors to express the temporary nature of their power - like water that flows away, arrows that miss, or a slug melting as it moves. They seem dangerous, but their strength will soon dissolve.

David's cry may seem severe, but it is grounded in a deep longing for righteousness. *"The righteous will be glad when they are avenged, when they dip their feet in the blood of the wicked."* The Psalm concludes: *"Surely the righteous still are rewarded; surely there is a God who judges the earth."*

Key Verse: (v.11)
"Surely the righteous still are rewarded; surely there is a God who judges the earth."

Application:

Psalm 58 reminds us that God sees injustice and will not remain silent. In a world filled with corruption, deceit, and abuse of power, it is comforting to know that God is a just Judge. Even when earthly rulers fail, God's justice will prevail. Trust in Him, live righteously, and know that your hope is not in the systems of this world but in the judgment and reward of the Lord.

PSALM 59

Author: David

Theme: Confidence in God while under siege.

Summary:

Psalm 59 was written when Saul sent men to watch David's house in order to kill him (1 Samuel 19). David begins with an urgent cry: *"Deliver me from my enemies, O God; be my fortress against those who are attacking me."* His foes are relentless and unjust, yet David insists on his innocence: *"I have done no wrong, yet they are ready to attack me."*

Despite his desperate situation, David's tone shifts quickly. He mocks the futility of his enemies, comparing them to howling dogs prowling the city at night. *"But you laugh at them, Lord; you scoff at all those nations."* David takes comfort in the fact that God is not threatened by evil. He calls God his strength and refuge. *"You are my strength, I watch for you; you, God, are my fortress."* David's trust is not shaken. Though his enemies return each night like snarling dogs, he sings of God's love every morning. *"I will sing of your strength; in the morning I will sing of your love."*

David does not take vengeance into his own hands. He entrusts the outcome to God, asking that his enemies be brought down without total annihilation so that others may learn. He ends with praise: *"You are my fortress, my refuge in times of trouble."*

Key Verse: (v.16)
"But I will sing of your strength, in the morning I will sing of your love, for you are my fortress, my refuge in times of trouble."

Application:

Psalm 59 teaches us that God is our defender in the darkest nights. When you feel surrounded, watched, or pursued, you can still sing. Fear is real, but so is God's faithfulness. Keep your eyes on Him and let His strength be your song even before the battle is over. He will not fail you.

PSALM 60

Author: David

Theme: Crying out to God after defeat.

Summary:

Psalm 60 was written after a military setback when David's forces suffered loss before eventual victory. He opens with a lament: *"You have rejected us, God, and burst upon us; you have been angry - now restore us!"* David sees God's hand in the loss and does not hide from it.

He describes the disorientation of the people: *"You have shown your people desperate times; you have given us wine that makes us stagger."* Yet in the middle of distress, hope arises. *"But for those who fear you, you have raised a banner to be unfurled against the bow."* Even in hardship, God gives a sign of His presence.

David pleads, *"Save us and help us with your right hand, that those you love may be delivered."* He then affirms God's sovereignty over the land, declaring that every region - from Shechem to Moab - is under God's rule. *"To me Gilead belongs, and Manasseh... Judah is my sceptre."*

Though defeat stings, David knows that human strength is not the answer: *"Give us aid against the enemy, for human help is worthless."* The Psalm closes with confident resolve: *"With God we will gain the victory, and he will trample down our enemies."*

Key Verse: (v.12)
"With God we will gain the victory, and he will trample down our enemies."

Application:

Psalm 60 teaches us to seek God in both victory and defeat. Loss is not the end of the story when you walk with Him. Admit your struggles, acknowledge His sovereignty, and ask for His help. Human strength fails - but God never does. He turns setbacks into victories for those who call on Him.

PSALM 61

Author: David

Theme: Seeking refuge and strength in God.

Summary:

Psalm 61 opens with a heartfelt and urgent plea: *"Hear my cry, O God; listen to my prayer."* David is in a place of emotional and perhaps physical distance from Jerusalem, expressing his sense of isolation and longing for God's nearness. David's request is deeply personal: *"Lead me to the rock that is higher than I."* This rock symbolizes stability and salvation. It is a recognition that David cannot lift himself up; he needs God to do it.

His longing is not merely for safety but for intimacy with God. *"I long to dwell in your tent forever and take refuge in the shelter of your wings."* This imagery of wings evokes the cherubim over the Ark of the Covenant. David then turns his attention to the king, likely praying for his own reign. He asks God to *"increase the days of the king's life"* and extend his rule for generations. This intercession reveals David's understanding of leadership as dependent on divine favour, not personal strength.

He concludes with a vow of ongoing praise: *"Then will I ever sing in praise of your name and fulfill my vows day after day."* Even amid distress, David's instinct is to worship and recommit himself to God. His cry is not only for rescue but for a restored relationship that leads to lifelong devotion.

Key Verse: (v.2)

"Lead me to the rock that is higher than I."

Application:

Psalm 61 teaches us that God is our refuge when life overwhelms us. In moments of weakness or distance, we can call out to Him for strength and stability. He alone is the rock that lifts us higher. This Psalm encourages us to seek not only protection but ongoing communion with God. His presence is our shelter, and our response should be continual praise and faithful living.

PSALM 62

Author: David

Theme: Rest and confidence in God alone.

Summary:

Psalm 62 is a profound declaration of trust in God in the face of pressure and opposition. David begins, *"Truly my soul finds rest in God; my salvation comes from him."* This rest is not passive - it is an active, chosen confidence. David anchors himself in the truth that God alone is his rock, salvation, and fortress.

He contrasts his faith with the actions of those around him: enemies who *"want to topple me from my lofty place."* These people bless with their mouths but curse in their hearts. They appear friendly, yet their intentions are corrupt.

In response, David repeats and reinforces his faith: *"Yes, my soul, find rest in God; my hope comes from him."* David does not merely survive adversity; he thrives in trust. *"He is my fortress, I will not be shaken."* God is not just his refuge but also his hope.

David then reflects on the nature of humanity: whether lowborn or highborn, people are *"but a breath."* David concludes with theological clarity: *"One thing God has spoken, two things I have heard: Power belongs to you, God, and with you, Lord, is unfailing love."* These dual truths - God's sovereignty and God's love - sustain his confidence.

Key Verse: (v.1)

"Truly my soul finds rest in God; my salvation comes from him."

Application:

Psalm 62 reminds us that peace is not found in possessions, status, or human approval. It is found in the character of God - both powerful and loving. When you are under pressure, speak to your soul. Remind yourself where your hope lies. Pour out your heart to God, trust in His timing, and rest in His strength. He is the only foundation that will never be shaken.

PSALM 63

Author: David

Theme: Longing for God in the wilderness.

Summary:

Psalm 63 was written while David was in the Desert of Judah. It begins with a passionate cry: *"You, God, are my God, earnestly I seek you."* Far from the sanctuary, David feels spiritually parched. Despite his physical hardship, David reflects on past worship: *"I have seen you in the sanctuary and beheld your power and your glory."* Praise is not postponed until things improve. *"I will praise you as long as I live, and in your name I will lift up my hands."* Even in his suffering, David finds satisfaction in God: *"I will be fully satisfied as with the richest of foods."*

During the watches of the night, David meditates on God: *"On my bed I remember you; I think of you through the watches of the night."* The wilderness becomes a place of worship. *"Because you are my help, I sing in the shadow of your wings."* God's protection is real and intimate - like the covering wings of a bird.

David closes the Psalm with confidence. Though enemies pursue him, they will fall by the sword and become *"food for jackals."* He knows that God will act. Meanwhile, *"the king will rejoice in God; all who swear by God will glory in him."* The mouths of liars will be silenced.

Key Verse: (v.3)

"Because your love is better than life, my lips will glorify you."

Application:

Psalm 63 teaches us to seek God not just in comfort, but in hardship. Spiritual hunger is often most intense in dry seasons. When we are isolated, weary, or under pressure, we can still worship. God satisfies the soul, even in the wilderness. Let your longing for God grow into praise. Meditate on His power, glory, and love - especially when life feels barren.

PSALM 64

Author: David

Theme: God sees and judges the schemes of the wicked.

Summary:

Psalm 64 is a prayer for protection from the malicious and hidden attacks of enemies. David opens with urgency: *"Hear me, my God, as I voice my complaint; protect my life from the threat of the enemy."* This is not just physical danger - it includes emotional and reputational harm caused by deceitful, slanderous people.

David describes the weapon of choice: words. His adversaries *"sharpen their tongues like swords and aim cruel words like deadly arrows."* These enemies attack from the shadows. *"They shoot from ambush at the innocent; they shoot suddenly, without fear."* The Psalm captures the nature of evil: *"They encourage each other in evil plans, they talk about hiding their snares; they say, 'Who will see it?'"*

In a powerful turning point, the Psalm declares: *"But God will shoot them with his arrows; they will suddenly be struck down."* The irony is unmistakable - those who use words like weapons will be undone by divine justice. *"He will turn their own tongues against them and bring them to ruin."* Their downfall will be public and undeniable. The Psalm concludes with a word of hope and encouragement: *"The righteous will rejoice in the Lord and take refuge in him; all the upright in heart will glory in him."*

Key Verse: (v.7)

"But God will shoot them with his arrows; they will suddenly be struck down."

Application:

Psalm 64 is a reminder that God sees what is hidden. In a world where gossip, slander, and schemes can thrive behind closed doors, we may feel vulnerable or unfairly attacked. But God is not blind or passive. He hears our cries, defends the innocent, and brings justice in His time.

PSALM 65

Author: David

Theme: Praise for God's forgiveness,
power, and abundant provision.

Summary:

Psalm 65 is a song of celebration, moving from the temple courts to the farthest reaches of the earth, highlighting God's grace, power, and generosity. David begins, *"Praise awaits you, our God, in Zion; to you our vows will be fulfilled .."* then humanity's deepest need: forgiveness. *"When we were overwhelmed by sins, you forgave our transgressions."* This access to God's presence is the highest privilege, and David rejoices in the satisfaction it brings: *"We are filled with the good things of your house, of your holy temple."*

The Psalm then shifts to focus on God's power over creation and nations. *"You answer us with awesome and righteous deeds, God our Saviour, the hope of all the ends of the earth."* David proclaims that God formed the mountains by His strength and stills the roaring seas. These images convey physical might but also God's ability to calm global unrest. David then marvels at God's provision, describing the earth as cared for like a garden: *"You care for the land and water it… you soften it with showers and bless its crops."*

Key Verse: (v.11)

"You crown the year with your bounty, and your carts overflow with abundance."

Application:

Psalm 65 reminds us that God is not only the Redeemer of souls but also the Sustainer of creation. He forgives our sins, welcomes us into His presence, and faithfully provides for our needs. In times of lack or uncertainty, we can reflect on His past provision and trust Him for the future. Worship is not only for spiritual blessings but also for the beauty and abundance of the world He sustains. Let creation's joy become your own as you praise the God who satisfies both soul and soil.

PSALM 66

Author: Unknown

Theme: Praising God for His mighty deeds
and faithfulness through trials.

Summary:
Psalm 66 is a communal hymn of praise, calling all the earth to
worship the greatness of God. *"Shout for joy to God, all the earth!
Sing the glory of his name; make his praise glorious!"* The Psalm then
offers an historical reflection. *"Come and see what God has done, his
awesome deeds for mankind!"* This is followed by praise for His
sovereignty.

Verses 8 to 12 highlight God's faithfulness through trial. *"Praise
our God, all peoples... he has preserved our lives."* Yet, the Psalm
does not ignore suffering. *"You tested us, God; you refined us like
silver."* God allowed them to be burdened and oppressed, but He
also brought them out to a place of abundance. The Psalmist then
shifts from communal to personal reflection. *"I will come to your
temple with burnt offerings... I will sacrifice fat animals to you."*
These acts are in fulfillment of vows made during trouble.

The closing verses speak of God's attentiveness to prayer. *"Come
and hear, all you who fear God; let me tell you what he has done for
me."*

Key Verse: (v.5)
"Come and see what God has done, his awesome deeds for mankind!"

Application:
Psalm 66 invites us to reflect on God's goodness both in triumph
and in testing. When we look back on the ways God has
delivered us, we are moved to praise. And when we pass
through fire and water, we remember that He refines, not
forsakes. Share your testimony - what God has done for you may
be exactly what someone else needs to hear. Worship God in
public and in private, with your voice and your life.

PSALM 67

Author: Unknown

Theme: God's blessing for His people and His global mission.

Summary:

Psalm 67 is a short but rich prayer for God's blessing, rooted in a global vision. It begins, *"May God be gracious to us and bless us and make his face shine on us."* This echoes the priestly blessing of Numbers 6:24–26, but it goes further - it ties blessing to mission.

The Psalm celebrates the joy that comes when people know and worship God. *"May the peoples praise you, God; may all the peoples praise you."* This repeated refrain anchors the Psalm's central desire: that God would be glorified in all the earth. The emphasis on God's just leadership is important. The Psalmist doesn't seek dominance but righteousness.

In verses 6 and 7, the Psalm turns to gratitude for physical provision. *"The land yields its harvest; God, our God, blesses us."* The blessing of the land is tied to the recognition that all good things come from God. It's not a self-sufficient prosperity, but one that acknowledges God as the giver.

The final verse repeats the purpose of blessing: *"May God bless us still, so that all the ends of the earth will fear him."* The fear of God here is reverent awe, a recognition of His majesty and mercy. The Psalm circles back to its beginning, tying blessing to mission.

Key Verse: (vv.1-2)

"May God be gracious to us and bless us and make his face shine on us - so that your ways may be known on earth."

Application:

Psalm 67 reminds us that God blesses His people not only for their good but for His glory. As you experience His grace, ask how it might be used to point others to Him. Whether through generosity, testimony, or missions, your blessing is a conduit for His name to be known. Seek God's face not just for personal gain, but for the sake of the world.

PSALM 68

Author: David

Theme: God's victorious power and His care for His people.

Summary:

Psalm 68 is a triumphant declaration of God's sovereign power, His faithfulness to Israel, and His care for the vulnerable. It begins with the powerful invocation, *"May God arise, may his enemies be scattered; may his foes flee before him."* The Psalm quickly moves to contrast: while the wicked perish, *"the righteous are glad and rejoice before God."* David invites the people to praise the One who is *"a father to the fatherless, a defender of widows."* These descriptions emphasize both the majesty and mercy of God.

As the Psalm progresses, David describes God's victories over kings and enemies. *"The Lord announces the word, and the women who proclaim it are a mighty throng."* He makes His dwelling in Zion, choosing it as His resting place forever: *"This is my dwelling forever and ever; here I will live, for I have desired it."* Verse 18, which Paul later applies to Christ in Ephesians 4, declares, *"When you ascended on high, you took many captives."* This adds a prophetic dimension, pointing to Jesus.

The Psalm ends with a call to praise the God who rides *"on the ancient skies,"* who *"gives power and strength to his people."*

Key Verse: (v.19)
"Praise be to the Lord, to God our Savior, who daily bears our burdens."

Application:

Psalm 68 invites us to worship the God who reigns in glory and walks with the needy. He leads, provides, defends, and empowers. Let this Psalm strengthen your confidence - your God is not passive. He is a mighty warrior and a compassionate Father. Praise Him for past victories, trust Him in present trials, and celebrate His eternal reign.

PSALM 69

Author: David

Theme: A cry for mercy in the midst of unjust suffering.

Summary:

Psalm 69 is one of David's most heartfelt laments and is also one of the most quoted Psalms in the New Testament. It begins with desperation: *"Save me, O God, for the waters have come up to my neck."* David feels overwhelmed by his circumstances. He is physically exhausted and emotionally drained: *"I am worn out calling for help; my throat is parched."* His troubles are also compounded by slander and betrayal: *"Those who hate me without reason outnumber the hairs of my head."*

David's zeal for God has made him a target. *"Zeal for your house consumes me,"* a verse applied to Jesus Christ in John 2:17. This connection between David's experience and Christ's passion reveals a prophetic layer to the Psalm. Despite his anguish, he continues to seek God: *"But I pray to you, Lord, in the time of your favour; in your great love, answer me."*

David then shifts focus to God's justice. He prays that his enemies will be exposed and judged. Yet even in his appeals for justice, he maintains a posture of humility. *"I am in pain and distress; may your salvation, God, protect me."* The Psalm ends in renewed hope. *"I will praise God's name in song and glorify him with thanksgiving."*

Key Verse: (v.13)

"But I pray to you, Lord, in the time of your favour; in your great love, O God, answer me with your sure salvation."

Application:

Psalm 69 reminds us that it's okay to bring our raw emotions to God. He is not offended by our pain or confusion. Whether you are suffering unjustly or carrying deep sorrow, cry out to the God who hears. Trust in His timing and rest in His compassion.

PSALM 70

Author: David

Theme: A short and urgent prayer for help.

Summary:

Psalm 70 is a brief but powerful cry for help, almost identical to Psalm 40:13–17. It begins with urgency: *"Hasten, O God, to save me; come quickly, Lord, to help me."* There's no poetic flourish - just an appeal to God's nearness and aid in a time of distress. David asks that those who seek his harm be put to shame. *"May those who want to take my life be put to shame and confusion; may all who desire my ruin be turned back in disgrace."* He is not praying out of vengeance but asking for justice and divine intervention.

In contrast, David wants those who seek God to be filled with joy. *"But may all who seek you rejoice and be glad in you."* The repetition of *"may those who long for your saving help always say, 'The Lord is great!'"* reveals David's desire for God's glory even as he prays for rescue. The most poignant moment comes in verse 5: *"But as for me, I am poor and needy; come quickly to me, O God."* David's humility is palpable. He doesn't rely on his strength, status, or past victories. He confesses his need plainly, trusting in God's sufficiency.

The Psalm closes with reassurance: *"You are my help and my deliverer; Lord, do not delay."* It's a reminder that prayer doesn't have to be long to be effective. Sincerity and dependence are what matter most.

Key Verse: (v.5)

"But as for me, I am poor and needy; come quickly to me, O God."

Application:

Psalm 70 teaches us that urgent, honest prayers are welcomed by God. When in crisis, we can speak plainly, and trust deeply. God is not distant or disinterested. He is our deliverer. Whether your trouble is overwhelming or momentary, don't hesitate - call on Him now. The Lord is great, and He is near.

PSALM 71

Author: Unknown (traditionally attributed to David)

Theme: Lifelong trust in God's faithfulness.

Summary:

Psalm 71 is a deeply personal prayer reflecting on a life of faith. It opens with confidence: *"In you, Lord, I have taken refuge; let me never be put to shame."* The Psalmist has trusted in God from youth and now, in old age, continues to depend on Him. He calls on God to be his *"rock of refuge,"* a phrase rich with meaning, God is both a shelter and a steady foundation.

What makes this Psalm especially moving is its focus on aging. *"Do not cast me away when I am old; do not forsake me when my strength is gone."* The vulnerability of advancing years does not lead to despair but to deeper reliance on God's ongoing presence. He recalls God's sustaining hand from birth: *"From birth I have relied on you... I will ever praise you."* His trust is not theoretical; it's built on a history of divine faithfulness.

As the Psalm progresses, there is a vow to proclaim God's mighty acts to the next generation: *"Even when I am old and grey, do not forsake me, my God, till I declare your power to the next generation."* His hope is not just survival but testimony. The Psalm closes with expectation: *"You will increase my honour and comfort me once more."* Praise will be the final word. *"My lips will shout for joy when I sing praise to you – I, whom you have delivered."*

Key Verse: (v.18)

"Even when I am old and grey, do not forsake me, my God, till I declare your power to the next generation."

Application:

Psalm 71 reminds us that trust in God is not seasonal - it's for life. Whether you are young or aging, God remains the same rock of refuge. This Psalm calls us to proclaim His great faithfulness, especially as we grow older. Share your story, pass on your faith, and find fresh strength in the God.

PSALM 72

Author: Solomon (or a prayer of David for Solomon)

Theme: A prayer for the king's righteous rule and eternal reign.

Summary:

Psalm 72 is a royal Psalm, written by Solomon or composed by David as a prayer for his son's reign. It begins: *"Endow the king with your justice, O God, the royal son with your righteousness."* It is not just a wish for political success, but for godly leadership that reflects divine values. Justice is central. *"May he judge your people in righteousness, your afflicted ones with justice."*

The prayer moves into poetic imagery: *"May he be like rain falling on a mown field."* The king's influence should bring renewal and peace. His reign is hoped to be vast: *"May he rule from sea to sea and from the River to the ends of the earth."* Psalm 72 includes striking messianic overtones. The Psalmist speaks about foreign kings bringing tribute and all nations serving him. *"May all kings bow down to him and all nations serve him."* These verses reach past Solomon to the future King, Jesus Christ, whose kingdom truly spans all nations.

The Psalm ends in doxology: *"Praise be to the Lord God, the God of Israel, who alone does marvellous deeds."* It concludes Book II of the Psalms with reverent praise and a longing for the eternal reign of the righteous King.

Key Verse: (v.12)

"For he will deliver the needy who cry out, the afflicted who have no one to help."

Application:

Psalm 72 points us toward Jesus, the perfect King who rules with righteousness and compassion. As we long for justice in our world, we're reminded that His kingdom brings peace, equity, and restoration. Pray for leaders to reflect His heart, and trust that His reign will one day be fully realized. In Christ, the needy are lifted, and the nations are blessed.

PSALM 73

Author: Asaph

Theme: Finding true perspective in the presence of God.

Summary:

Psalm 73 opens with a theological declaration: *"Surely God is good to Israel, to those who are pure in heart."* Yet Asaph confesses that he nearly lost his footing because of envy. *"But as for me, my feet had almost slipped... for I envied the arrogant."* The Psalm is a journey from doubt to clarity. He describes how the wicked appear to prosper: *"They have no struggles, their bodies are healthy and strong."* This creates a crisis: *"Surely in vain I have kept my heart pure."* Asaph wonders if righteousness is worth it.

However, everything changes in verse 17: *"Till I entered the sanctuary of God; then I understood their final destiny."* The presence of God restores perspective. The apparent success of the wicked is fleeting. *"Surely you place them on slippery ground... they are destroyed in a moment."* Asaph realizes he had become bitter, yet God had not let go. *"Yet I am always with you; you hold me by my right hand."* God's nearness is his true treasure. *"Whom have I in heaven but you? And earth has nothing I desire besides you."*

The Psalm ends with a strong affirmation of faith: *"My flesh and my heart may fail, but God is the strength of my heart and my portion forever."* Justice will be done in the end, and the nearness of God is his lasting good.

Key Verse: (v.28)
"But as for me, it is good to be near God."

Application:

Psalm 73 is for anyone who has wrestled with why the wicked prosper while the faithful suffer. The answer is not found in circumstance but in God's presence. Draw near to Him. Let the sanctuary - a place of worship and truth - restore your whole perspective. God is your portion, and eternity will reveal His perfect justice.

PSALM 74

Author: Asaph

Theme: Lament over national ruin and a
plea for God's intervention.

Summary:

Psalm 74 is a national lament, likely written after the destruction
of the temple. It begins with a heartbreaking question: *"Why have
you rejected us forever, O God? Why does your anger smoulder against
the sheep of your pasture?"* Asaph feels the weight of divine silence
and devastation. He calls on God to remember His people. *"Turn
your steps toward these everlasting ruins, all this destruction the
enemy has brought on the sanctuary."*

Asaph describes the scene with anguish: enemies roared in the
sacred place and set up their standards. They smashed the
entrance and burned the sanctuary to the ground. *"They said in
their hearts, 'We will crush them completely!'"* It feels as though all
hope is gone.

Yet Asaph turns to remembrance. He recalls God's power in
creation - dividing the sea, crushing Leviathan, opening springs
and streams. These are reminders that God has acted in mighty
ways before. The final verses are a plea: *"Do not hand over the life
of your dove to wild beasts… Rise up, O God, and defend your cause."*
Asaph appeals to God's covenant and honour. His name has
been mocked, and the Psalmist begs Him to act for His glory.

Key Verse: (v.12)

*"But God is my King from long ago; he brings salvation
on the earth."*

Application:

Psalm 74 gives voice to the pain of feeling abandoned and the
fear that God is silent. In such seasons, remember who God has
always been. Remind Him - and yourself - of His covenant
faithfulness. Though destruction surrounds you, God remains
King. Hold fast to His power and His promises.

PSALM 75

Author: Asaph

Theme: God is the righteous judge.

Summary:

Psalm 75 opens with thanksgiving: *"We praise you, God, we praise you, for your Name is near."* God's name represents His presence and character, and His nearness brings confidence. The Psalm immediately affirms that God is the one who will *"judge with equity."* God Himself speaks in the Psalm, declaring, *"When the earth and all its people quake, it is I who hold its pillars firm."* The world may seem unstable, but God sustains it. He rebukes the arrogant and warns the wicked not to boast or lift up their horns - a symbol of power and pride.

Verse 6 clarifies the source of promotion or downfall: *"No one from the east or the west or from the desert can exalt themselves. It is God who judges."* He brings down one and exalts another. Human authority is ultimately subject to God's sovereign will.

The image of the cup appears next: *"In the hand of the Lord is a cup full of foaming wine mixed with spices."* This cup represents God's judgment. The wicked will be forced to drink it down to the dregs - there is no escaping divine justice. Asaph ends with a personal vow: *"As for me, I will declare this forever; I will sing praise to the God of Jacob."* He trusts that the horns of the wicked will be cut off, while the righteous will be lifted up.

Key Verse: (v.7)

"It is God who judges: He brings one down, he exalts another."

Application:

Psalm 75 reminds us that God alone is the righteous judge. When we see corruption or arrogance flourishing, we must remember who holds ultimate authority. Promotion and justice are not determined by chance or human effort, but by God's hand. Live humbly, trust His timing, and continue to praise the One who holds the world steady.

PSALM 76

Author: Asaph

Theme: God's awesome power and judgment.

Summary:

Psalm 76 is a celebration of God's power and justice, especially in Zion. It opens with a declaration: *"God is renowned in Judah; in Israel his name is great."* The Psalmist describes how God breaks the weapons of war: *"There he broke the flashing arrows, the shields and the swords, the weapons of war."* God is portrayed as majestic and awe-inspiring, more powerful than any earthly army. *"You are radiant with light, more majestic than mountains rich with game."*

What follows is a dramatic account of God's judgment. The brave warriors of the enemy are plundered and sleep the sleep of death. *"No one of the warriors can lift his hands."* The Psalmist is clear: *"You alone are to be feared. Who can stand before you when you are angry?"* God's judgment is not random but righteous. *"From heaven you pronounced judgment, and the land feared and was quiet - when you, God, rose up to judge, to save all the afflicted of the land."* His justice brings peace and deliverance to the oppressed.

The Psalm ends with a call to respond. *"Make vows to the Lord your God and fulfill them."* Even the powerful are urged to bring tribute to the One who is truly sovereign. *"He breaks the spirit of rulers; he is feared by the kings of the earth."*

Key Verse: (v.7)
"You alone are to be feared. Who can stand before you when you are angry?"

Application:

Psalm 76 reminds us that God is not to be taken lightly. He is a warrior and a judge, righteous and sovereign. When we witness injustice or feel overwhelmed by the power of this world, we must remember that no ruler, army, or system stands above God. Honour Him with reverence and trust Him to always act justly.

PSALM 77

Author: Asaph

Theme: From despair to hope.

Summary:

Psalm 77 begins with a cry from the depths of despair. *"I cried out to God for help; I cried out to God to hear me."* The Psalmist is restless and troubled. *"You kept my eyes from closing; I was too troubled to speak."* He remembers God but feels overwhelmed. In the night, he ponders painful questions: *"Will the Lord reject forever? Will he never show his favour again?"* He wonders whether God's promises have failed and whether His compassion has vanished. These raw questions show the depth of his anguish.

But the turning point comes in verse 11: *"I will remember the deeds of the Lord; yes, I will remember your miracles of long ago."* Asaph shifts his focus from present pain to past faithfulness. He reflects on God's wonders, power, and holiness. The central example is the Exodus. *"Your path led through the sea, your way through the mighty waters, though your footprints were not seen."* God made a way where there was none, delivering His people and showing that He's a God who saves.

This deliberate shift from despair to remembrance does not erase the pain, but it reframes it. Asaph ends by affirming God's leadership: *"You led your people like a flock by the hand of Moses and Aaron."* The image is pastoral - God delivers, but He also guides.

Key Verse: (v.11)

"I will remember the deeds of the Lord; yes, I will remember your miracles of long ago."

Application:

Psalm 77 teaches us the value of remembering. When God seems distant, recall His past faithfulness. Your feelings may waver, but His record stands firm. In seasons of silence or sorrow, shift your focus from what hurts to what helps - God's unchanging power and grace. Let memory lead you back to hope.

PSALM 78

Author: Asaph

Theme: Passing on God's works and a
warning against forgetfulness.

Summary:

Psalm 78 is one of the longest Psalms, offering a sweeping history
of Israel's relationship with God. It begins with a call to teach
future generations: *"We will not hide them from their descendants;
we will tell the next generation the praiseworthy deeds of the Lord."*
Teaching is both a duty and a legacy. The Psalm recounts God's
mighty works - the Exodus, the parting of the sea, the provision
of manna and water. But it also recounts Israel's repeated failure
to trust and obey. *"They forgot what he had done, the wonders he had
shown them."*

Despite miracles, the people grumbled and sinned. *"In spite of all
this, they kept on sinning."* God's anger burned, yet His mercy
remained. He *"did not destroy them completely,"* showing great
compassion. The Psalm reminds us how forgetfulness leads to
rebellion. It details the failure of Ephraim, the rejection of Shiloh,
and finally the rise of David. *"He chose David his servant and took
him from the sheep pens... to be the shepherd of his people."*

Psalm 78 serves as both a warning and an encouragement:
remember God's works and walk in His ways.

Key Verse: (v.4)

*"We will not hide them from their descendants; we will tell the next
generation the praiseworthy deeds of the Lord."*

Application:

Psalm 78 challenges us to be faithful storytellers of God's grace.
Teach your children, your community, and yourself what God
has done. Memory is a spiritual discipline. When we remember,
we remain grounded. When we forget, we drift. Guard against
spiritual amnesia and pass on the legacy of faith.

PSALM 79

Author: Asaph

Theme: Lament over destruction and plea for mercy.

Summary:

Psalm 79 is a lament over the devastation of Jerusalem, likely written after the Babylonian destruction. It opens with stark imagery: *"O God, the nations have invaded your inheritance; they have defiled your holy temple."* The dead are left unburied, and the city is in ruins.

The Psalmist acknowledges the scorn of surrounding nations: *"We are objects of contempt to our neighbours."* There is deep sorrow, but also a cry for divine response. *"How long, Lord? Will you be angry forever?"*

He pleads for forgiveness - not on the basis of Israel's merit but on God's mercy. *"Do not hold against us the sins of past generations; may your mercy come quickly to meet us, for we are in desperate need."*

The Psalm calls for justice, asking God to repay the nations that have brought destruction, but the ultimate focus is on God's reputation: *"Help us, God our Savior, for the glory of your name."* It ends with a vow of praise: *"Then we your people, the sheep of your pasture, will praise you forever."* Even in grief, worship is the response.

Key Verse: (v.9)

"Help us, God our Savior, for the glory of your name; deliver us and forgive our sins for your name's sake."

Application:

Psalm 79 reminds us to turn to God in national and personal crisis. When we are overwhelmed by loss or surrounded by scorn, our refuge is still in Him. Pray not just for relief, but for the restoration of God's name among His people. Even in ruins, worship leads us home.

PSALM 80

Author: Asaph

Theme: A plea for restoration and renewed favour.

Summary:

Psalm 80 is a prayer for national renewal, addressed to the *"Shepherd of Israel."* It begins with urgency: *"Hear us, Shepherd of Israel… awaken your might; come and save us."* The refrain appears three times: *"Restore us, O God; make your face shine on us, that we may be saved."* The Psalm laments God's apparent rejection: *"You have fed them with the bread of tears."* The people feel broken and vulnerable, mocked by neighbours and torn down like a ruined vineyard. *"Your vine is cut down… your people perish at your rebuke."*

The image of the vine is central. God had brought Israel out of Egypt and planted them in the land like a flourishing vine. But now the walls are broken, and wild animals trample it. This vivid imagery captures the devastation and longing for divine intervention.

The Psalm shifts to hope. *"Let your hand rest on the man at your right hand,"* a probable reference to the king or even messianic prophecy. The people cry out for renewed life and commitment: *"Then we will not turn away from you; revive us, and we will call on your name."* The repeated refrain is a prayer of repentance and longing: *"Restore us, Lord God Almighty; make your face shine on us, that we may be saved."*

Key Verse: (v.19)
"Restore us, Lord God Almighty; make your face shine on us, that we may be saved."

Application:

Psalm 80 is a model for prayer in times of decline. When life or ministry feels broken, cry out for restoration. Ask God to revive what once flourished. His face shining on us is our hope, not our performance or strength. Trust Him to renew what has been lost.

PSALM 81

Author: Asaph

Theme: A call to celebrate God and listen to His voice.

Summary:

Psalm 81 opens with celebration: *"Sing for joy to God our strength; shout aloud to the God of Jacob!"* The people are called to worship with instruments. The Psalm recalls how God delivered Israel from Egypt, making this a song of both joy and remembrance. It speaks of a divine ordinance established by God: *"He established it as a statute for Joseph when he went out against Egypt."* Asaph recalls God's voice during that time of deliverance: *"I removed the burden from their shoulders; their hands were set free from the basket."*

However, the tone shifts as God laments Israel's disobedience: *"But my people would not listen to me; Israel would not submit to me."* God allowed them to follow their stubborn hearts. This reveals the tension in the covenant relationship - God desires obedience, not just ritual worship.

Despite their failure, God's longing remains clear: *"If my people would only listen to me, if Israel would only follow my ways."* His desire is to bless: *"I would quickly subdue their enemies... you would be fed with the finest of wheat; with honey from the rock I would satisfy you."* This Psalm captures both divine joy and divine grief - a celebration of God's faithfulness, and a lament over His people's failure to listen.

Key Verse: (vv.13-14)
"If my people would only listen to me... how quickly I would subdue their enemies."

Application:

Psalm 81 calls us not only to sing but to submit. Worship must be matched with obedience. God longs to bless, but our hearts must be open to His leading. Take time to reflect - are you listening to God, or just singing to Him? True joy comes when praise and obedience walk hand in hand.

PSALM 82

Author: Asaph

Theme: God judges unjust rulers.

Summary:

Psalm 82 presents a courtroom scene. God is pictured presiding over a divine council: *"God presides in the great assembly; he renders judgment among the 'gods.'"* These "gods" are likely earthly rulers or judges - those given authority to represent God's justice. God rebukes them for failing in their duty: *"How long will you defend the unjust and show partiality to the wicked?"* Instead of upholding justice, they have sided with the corrupt. The charge is specific: *"Defend the weak and the fatherless; uphold the cause of the poor and the oppressed."*

God's frustration is clear. These leaders lack understanding: *"The 'gods' know nothing, they walk about in darkness."* As a result, the foundations of society are shaken - when justice is neglected, everything suffers. Despite their status, God declares their mortality: *"You are 'gods'; you are all sons of the Most High. But you will die like mere mortals."* Their authority is not immunity. An accountability is coming.

The Psalm ends with a plea: *"Rise up, O God, judge the earth, for all the nations are your inheritance."* When human justice fails, we cry out for divine intervention.

Key Verse: (v.3)
"Defend the weak and the fatherless; uphold the cause of the poor and the oppressed."

Application:

Psalm 82 reminds us that authority is a trust, not a privilege. Whether in leadership, influence, or judgment, we are always accountable to God. Are you using your position to defend the vulnerable or protect the powerful? God sees every injustice and will judge rightly. Stand with the weak - because He does.

PSALM 83

Author: Asaph

Theme: A prayer for deliverance from national enemies.

Summary:

Psalm 83 is a passionate plea for God to act against Israel's enemies. *"O God, do not remain silent; do not turn a deaf ear, do not stand aloof."* The Psalmist is troubled by a growing coalition against God's people. *"Your enemies make a commotion; those who hate you have raised their heads."* Ten nations are listed, forming a confederacy with the goal: *"Come, let us destroy them as a nation, so that Israel's name is remembered no more."* This is not just opposition - it is annihilation. The threat is real, and the Psalmist responds with urgent intercession.

He appeals to past victories: *"Do to them as you did to Midian… to Sisera and Jabin."* These references remind God - and the people - of His past faithfulness in delivering Israel from overwhelming odds. The Psalmist asks God to drive the enemies like chaff before the wind, to terrify and shame them so they may seek His name. This is more than vengeance - it's a call for God's justice to lead even enemies to acknowledge Him.

It ends with a powerful prayer: *"Let them know that you, whose name is the Lord – that you alone are the Most High over all the earth."* The Psalm is both a battle cry and a call for recognition of God's supreme authority.

Key Verse: (v.18)
"Let them know that you, whose name is the Lord - that you alone are the Most High over all the earth."

Application:

Psalm 83 shows us how to pray in the face of opposition. When forces rise against God's people, our hope is not in numbers or strategies, but in divine intervention. God has done it before - and He can again. Let your cries be bold, and your faith be rooted in His sovereignty.

PSALM 84

Author: Sons of Korah

Theme: The joy of dwelling in God's presence.

Summary:

Psalm 84 is a radiant expression of longing for communion with God. *"How lovely is your dwelling place, Lord Almighty!"* The Psalmist's entire being - soul, heart, and flesh - yearns for the courts of the Lord. Even birds are at home near God's altar: *"Even the sparrow has found a home, and the swallow a nest for herself... a place near your altar."*

In His house, even the smallest and most overlooked creatures find refuge and rest. *"Blessed are those who dwell in your house; they are ever praising you."* Those who live in continual fellowship with God are constantly filled with praise.

The Psalm shifts to address pilgrims - those journeying to worship. *"Blessed are those whose strength is in you, whose hearts are set on pilgrimage."* Even as they pass through the dry Valley of Baka, they make it a place of springs. The journey of faith transforms hardship into blessing. *"They go from strength to strength, till each appears before God in Zion."*

A heartfelt prayer follows: *"Hear my prayer, Lord God Almighty; listen to me, God of Jacob."* The Psalmist pleads for God's favour and protection: *"Look on our shield, O God; look with favour on your anointed one."* Then comes one of Scripture's most treasured statements, and the key verse in this Psalm:

Key Verse: (v.10)

"Better is one day in your courts than a thousand elsewhere."

Application:

Psalm 84 challenges us to realign our priorities. Do we value the presence of God above everything else? In a world of constant distractions, this Psalm reminds us that nearness to God is the greatest joy and safest refuge. Make time to dwell with Him - through worship, prayer, and daily communion.

PSALM 85

Author: Sons of Korah

Theme: A prayer for revival and restoration.

Summary:

Psalm 85 opens with a look back: *"You, Lord, showed favour to your land; you restored the fortunes of Jacob."* The Psalmist remembers when God forgave the people, covered their sin, withdrew His wrath, and turned from fierce anger. The community pleads, *"Restore us again, God our Saviour. Will you not revive us again, that your people may rejoice in you?"* There is deep awareness of current spiritual decline but also hope rooted in God's proven character.

The Psalmist continues, *"Show us your unfailing love, Lord, and grant us your salvation."* The speaker listens intently for God's response: *"I will listen to what God the Lord says; he promises peace to his people."* Yet this peace is conditional upon their return: *"but let them not return to folly."* The central image of the Psalm is poetic and profound: *"Love and faithfulness meet together; righteousness and peace kiss each other."* God's justice and mercy, often seen as opposites, are united in His redemptive work. *"Faithfulness springs forth from the earth, and righteousness looks down from heaven."*

The final line points toward a faithful walk: *"Righteousness goes before him and prepares the way for his steps."* When God restores His people, it leads to a path of justice and flourishing.

Key Verse: (v.4)

"Restore us again, God our Saviour… that your people may rejoice in you."

Application:

Psalm 85 speaks to every generation that longs for revival. Have you known God's touch in the past but now feel dry or distant? This Psalm invites us to remember, repent, and return. God delights to restore. He longs for us to walk in righteousness and enjoy His peace.

PSALM 86

Author: David

Theme: A humble prayer for mercy, guidance, and strength.

Summary:

Psalm 86 is a deeply personal and humble prayer from David, who begins by pleading, *"Hear me, Lord, and answer me, for I am poor and needy."* David appeals to God's character: *"You are my God; have mercy on me, Lord, for I call to you all day long."* He knows that God is *"forgiving and good, abounding in love to all who call to you."* These attributes are the foundation of his trust and hope.

The Psalm moves between requests and declarations. David asks for joy: *"Bring joy to your servant, Lord, for I put my trust in you."* He pleads for God's attention and calls on Him in trouble. Then he shifts to praise: *"Among the gods there is none like you, Lord... For you are great and do marvellous deeds; you alone are God."*

David then makes a beautiful request: *"Teach me your way, Lord, that I may rely on your faithfulness."* He doesn't just want rescue — he desires transformation. His goal is worship: *"I will praise you, Lord my God, with all my heart."* There's also urgency. David is surrounded by enemies, *"a ruthless mob."* But even in fear, he returns to God's compassion: *"But you, Lord, are a compassionate and gracious God, slow to anger, abounding in love and faithfulness."* The final plea is bold yet humble: *"Give me a sign of your goodness."* David is not demanding proof for his own sake, but so his enemies will know that God is with him.

Key Verse: (v.11)

"Teach me your way, Lord, that I may rely on your faithfulness."

Application:

Psalm 86 teaches us how to pray when we're in need. Come honestly, acknowledging your weakness and God's greatness. Lean into His character - He is compassionate, faithful, and willing to respond. Don't just seek help - seek holiness. Ask God to teach you His ways.

PSALM 87

Author: Sons of Korah

Theme: The glory of God's city and the inclusion of the nations.

Summary:

Psalm 87 is a brief but profound meditation on Zion - the city of God. It begins with celebration: *"He has founded his city on the holy mountain. The Lord loves the gates of Zion more than all the other dwellings of Jacob."* This city represents more than geography - it's the centre of God's redemptive plan.

Then the Psalmist declares, *"Glorious things are said of you, city of God."* This isn't about military strength or architectural grandeur - it's about divine purpose. But what follows is surprising: *"I will record Rahab and Babylon among those who acknowledge me - Philistia too, and Tyre, along with Cush - and will say, 'This one was born in Zion.'"* These are historical enemies of Israel, yet they are now counted among God's people.

The Psalm envisions a future when people from all nations will be joined to God's covenant community. *"Indeed, of Zion it will be said, 'This one and that one were born in her, and the Most High himself will establish her.'"* This is not just about ancestry - it's also about spiritual rebirth and divine inclusion. The Lord Himself will write the register of the peoples, affirming their place in His city. The Psalm ends with celebration: *"As they make music they will sing, 'All my fountains are in you.'"*

Key Verse: (v.6)

"The Lord will write in the register of the peoples: 'This one was born in Zion.'"

Application:

Psalm 87 points us to the inclusive beauty of God's kingdom. People from every nation can be reborn into the city of God. It's not about heritage - it's about grace. Rejoice that you belong to a heavenly Zion, and welcome others into that joy. Our identity is not in where we're from, but in who we belong to.

PSALM 88

Author: Heman the Ezrahite

Theme: A raw and honest cry from the depths of despair.

Summary:

Psalm 88 is one of the most sombre and emotionally raw Psalms in the Bible. It opens: *"Lord, you are the God who saves me; day and night I cry out to you."* Despite this acknowledgment of God's power to save, the tone quickly plunges into deep lament.

Heman describes his life as full of troubles: *"I am overwhelmed with troubles and my life draws near to death."* He feels like one forgotten by God, lying among the dead. *"You have put me in the lowest pit,"* he laments. *"Your wrath lies heavily on me."* The Psalmist attributes his suffering directly to God, yet he continues to pray. This tension - complaint within relationship - is a key to biblical lament.

He also speaks of isolation: *"You have taken from me my closest friends."* He is shunned, trapped, and blinded by sorrow. *"From my youth I have suffered and been close to death,"* he says, showing that his pain is not fleeting - it's lifelong.

What makes Psalm 88 unique is its ending. Unlike most laments, it doesn't resolve in hope or praise. The final line is haunting: *"Darkness is my closest friend."* Yet even here there's faith because the Psalmist is still praying, still crying out to the God who saves.

Key Verse: (v.1)

"Lord, you are the God who saves me; day and night I cry out to you."

Application:

Psalm 88 shows us that faith includes space for sorrow. When words fail and joy is distant, prayer is still possible. God welcomes our grief, even when we cannot see the way out. If darkness is your closest friend, know this: you are not alone. God hears - even in the silence.

PSALM 89

Author: Ethan the Ezrahite

Theme: God's covenant with David
and the pain of perceived failure.

Summary:

Psalm 89 begins with joyful confidence in God's promises: *"I will sing of the Lord's great love forever."* The Psalmist celebrates God's faithfulness and majesty, His power over creation, and His justice. *"Righteousness and justice are the foundation of your throne."* The heart of the Psalm centres on God's covenant with David: *"I have made a covenant with my chosen one... I will establish your line forever."* This promise of an eternal throne is affirmed repeatedly. David is described as God's servant, anointed and strengthened, protected from enemies.

But halfway through, the tone dramatically shifts. The Psalmist accuses God of abandoning the covenant: *"But you have rejected, you have spurned... You have renounced the covenant with your servant."* David's line appears broken, his crown defiled. The Psalmist struggles to reconcile God's promise with Israel's present humiliation. *"How long, Lord? Will you hide yourself forever?"* He pleads for God to remember His love and restore what has been lost.

Despite the despair, the final word is still praise: *"Praise be to the Lord forever! Amen and Amen."* The tension between promise and pain does not cancel worship.

Key Verse: (v.1)

"I will sing of the Lord's great love forever; with my mouth I will make your faithfulness known through all generations."

Application:

Psalm 89 teaches us to hold on when God's promises seem delayed. Life may look like contradiction, but God's covenant still stands. Even when the throne appears empty, the King is not gone. Keep singing of His love - even in the waiting.

PSALM 90

Author: Moses

Theme: God's eternal nature and man's frailty.

Summary:

Psalm 90 is the only Psalm attributed to Moses and reflects deep wisdom. It begins: *"Lord, you have been our dwelling place throughout all generations."* While human life is fleeting, God is eternal: *"Before the mountains were born... from everlasting to everlasting you are God."*

Moses contrasts God's timelessness with our mortality. *"You turn people back to dust."* A thousand years are like a day to God. Life is short - *"The length of our days is seventy years, or eighty, if we have the strength."* Even so, they are filled with trouble.

The Psalm acknowledges God's righteous anger over sin. *"We are consumed by your anger... our secret sins in the light of your presence."* This awareness leads to humility and a longing for wisdom.

Moses prays: *"Teach us to number our days, that we may gain a heart of wisdom."* He asks for compassion and satisfaction in God's love, that we may *"sing for joy and be glad all our days."* He concludes by asking God to establish the work of our hands, despite life's brevity, we long for our work to matter.

Key Verse: (v.12)

"Teach us to number our days, that we may gain a heart of wisdom."

Application:

Psalm 90 invites us to view life with eternal perspective. Time is limited - so live wisely. Acknowledge God's holiness, embrace His mercy, and ask Him to make your days meaningful. Even brief lives can have an eternal impact when they are guided by the hand of God.

PSALM 91

Author: Unknown

Theme: God's protection and deliverance.

Summary:

Psalm 91 is one of the most beloved declarations of God's protective care. It begins with a wonderful invitation to intimacy: *"Whoever dwells in the shelter of the Most High will rest in the shadow of the Almighty."* God is described with multiple names - Most High, Almighty, Lord, and God - emphasizing His sufficiency and strength.

The imagery is rich and personal. God will *"cover you with his feathers, and under his wings you will find refuge."* Just as a bird shelters its young, so God guards those who trust Him. *"His faithfulness will be your shield and rampart."*

The Psalm outlines the dangers one might face - pestilence, terror by night, arrows by day, plague, and disaster. Yet the faithful will be preserved: *"A thousand may fall at your side… but it will not come near you."* This is not a promise of trouble-free life, but assurance of God's sovereign care in the midst of trials.

God commands His angels to guard His people: "They will lift you up in their hands, so that you will not strike your foot against a stone." The Psalm reaches a climax as God Himself speaks, affirming His promise to protect, rescue, and satisfy those who love Him.

Key Verse: (v.4)
"He will cover you with his feathers, and under his wings you will find refuge."

Application:

Psalm 91 reminds us to make God our dwelling place. Life brings threats seen and unseen, but when we rest in Him, we are never alone. His protection may not always remove danger, but it surrounds us with peace and purpose. Trust in His presence - and rest under His wings.

PSALM 92

Theme: Praise for God's righteousness and faithfulness.

Summary:

Psalm 92 is titled *"A Psalm. A song for the Sabbath day,"* linking it directly with worship and rest. It opens with gratitude: *"It is good to praise the Lord and make music to your name, O Most High."* Giving thanks in the morning and proclaiming His faithfulness at night forms the rhythm of the believer's life.

The Psalmist reflects on God's deeds: *"For you make me glad by your deeds, Lord; I sing for joy at what your hands have done."* God's work is not just mighty - it's deeply personal, bringing joy.

In contrast to the joy of the righteous, the wicked seem to flourish temporarily. *"Though the wicked spring up like grass... they will be destroyed forever."* Their success is fleeting, but God is *"exalted forever."*

The righteous, by comparison, *"will flourish like a palm tree... planted in the house of the Lord."* Even in old age, they *"will still bear fruit, staying fresh and green."* This image highlights the enduring vitality that comes from living close to God.

The Psalm ends by affirming that *"The Lord is upright; he is my Rock, and there is no wickedness in him."* It is a declaration of trust in God's unchanging goodness.

Key Verse: (vv.12-13)
"The righteous will flourish like a palm tree... planted in the house of the Lord."

Application:
Psalm 92 encourages regular, joyful worship as a way of life. In every season - youth or old age - those deeply rooted in God will flourish. Don't envy the quick success of the wicked; stay planted in God's house. He is your rock, and your life will bear fruit.

PSALM 93

Author: Unknown

Theme: The majesty and eternal rule of God.

Summary:

Psalm 93 is a short yet powerful declaration of God's sovereign kingship. It opens triumphantly: *"The Lord reigns, he is robed in majesty; the Lord is robed in majesty and armed with strength."* This royal imagery emphasizes God's authority and power. He is not an idle ruler but engaged, clothed with strength and glory. The Psalm affirms the permanence of God's rule: *"The world is established, firm and secure. Your throne was established long ago; you are from all eternity."* In a world where so much seems fragile and uncertain, this declaration brings comfort.

The Psalm then turns to imagery of the sea: *"The seas have lifted up, Lord, the seas have lifted up their voice."* The Psalmist then acknowledges the might and noise of the waters but immediately contrasts it with God's greater power: *"Mightier than the thunder of the great waters… the Lord on high is mighty."* God's supremacy over the tumultuous sea is symbolic of His sovereignty over all forces of chaos and evil. Nothing threatens His reign.

The closing verse shifts the focus from power to holiness: *"Your statutes, Lord, stand firm; holiness adorns your house for endless days."* God's rule is not arbitrary or oppressive - it is marked by moral perfection.

Key Verse: (v.1)
"The Lord reigns, he is robed in majesty and armed with strength."

Application:

Psalm 93 anchors us in the truth that God is always in control. When the waves of life rise, threatening to overwhelm us, we can rest in the security of His eternal throne. His power is unmatched, and His rule is righteous. Trust in the one whose sovereignty is as ancient as eternity itself - and as steady as the earth beneath your feet.

PSALM 94

Author: Unknown

Theme: A call for God's justice in the face of oppression.

Summary:

Psalm 94 is a bold and passionate cry to the God of justice. It begins with urgency: *"The Lord is a God who avenges. O God who avenges, shine forth."* The Psalm describes the behaviour of the wicked: *"They crush your people, Lord; they oppress your inheritance. They slay the widow and the foreigner; they murder the fatherless."* These oppressors are not just immoral - they are destructive to the most vulnerable. Their arrogance is clear: *"The Lord does not see; the God of Jacob takes no notice."*

But the Psalmist challenges this foolishness: *"Does he who fashioned the ear not hear? Does he who formed the eye not see?"* The Creator is also the judge, and nothing escapes His attention. The Psalmist finds hope in God's discipline: *"Blessed is the one you discipline, Lord, the one you teach from your law."* He confidently declares that justice will return: *"Judgment will again be founded on righteousness, and all the upright in heart will follow it."* The Psalmist speaks from experience, saying, *"When I said, 'My foot is slipping,' your unfailing love, Lord, supported me."*

The Psalm ends with a powerful affirmation: *"The Lord has become my fortress, and my God the rock in whom I take refuge."* He knows that evil will not win. God will bring justice in His time.

Key Verse: (v.22)
"The Lord has become my fortress, and my God the rock in whom I take refuge."

Application:

Psalm 94 reminds us that we serve a God who sees every injustice and hears every cry. In an unjust world, we may feel tempted to despair, but God is still on the throne. He disciplines in love, strengthens the weary, and defends the oppressed. Rest in His justice and take refuge in His unfailing love.

PSALM 95

Author: Unknown

Theme: A call to worship and to listen to God's voice.

Summary:

Psalm 95 is both an invitation to joyful worship and a sober warning against disobedience. It begins with: *"Come, let us sing for joy to the Lord; let us shout aloud to the Rock of our salvation."* Worship is not just emotional - it's communal and full-hearted. The Psalm gives reasons for this joy: *"For the Lord is the great God, the great King above all gods."* God's greatness is seen in His creation. *"In his hand are the depths of the earth... the sea is his, for he made it."* Yet worship is also reverent: *"Come, let us bow down in worship, let us kneel before the Lord our Maker."* He is not only Creator but Shepherd. *"For he is our God and we are the people of his pasture, the flock under his care."* The imagery of the flock reveals God's tender, personal involvement with His people.

The second half turns into a prophetic warning: *"Today, if only you would hear his voice, do not harden your hearts as you did at Meribah."* God's frustration is evident: *"They are a people whose hearts go astray, and they have not known my ways."* His judgment follows: *"So I declared on oath in my anger, 'They shall never enter my rest.'"* This warning emphasizes the importance of obedient response to God's voice. Psalm 95 thus combines joyful praise with holy fear. It calls us to remember that the God we worship is also the God we must obey.

Key Verse: (vv.7-8)

"Today, if only you would hear his voice, do not harden your hearts."

Application:

Psalm 95 is a wake-up call to modern believers. Worship is not complete unless it includes obedience. God seeks worshippers who not only lift their voices in song but open their hearts in surrender. Do not delay. Hear His voice today and let your praise lead you to a life aligned with His will.

PSALM 96

Author: Unknown

Theme: A universal call to worship the Lord who reigns.

Summary:

Psalm 96 is a jubilant call to worship, inviting all nations to acknowledge the greatness of God. It begins: *"Sing to the Lord a new song; sing to the Lord, all the earth."* Every people group is called to praise.

The Psalm encourages proclamation: *"Declare his glory among the nations, his marvellous deeds among all peoples."* God is not one among many; He alone is worthy. *"For great is the Lord and most worthy of praise; he is to be feared above all gods."*

The Psalm contrasts the Lord with idols: *"For all the gods of the nations are idols, but the Lord made the heavens."* God is the Creator, majestic and powerful, and His sanctuary is marked by splendour and beauty. The nations are called to ascribe glory to God: *"Ascribe to the Lord, all you families of nations... bring an offering and come into his courts."* Worship is not only verbal - it's sacrificial and active. The earth is invited to tremble before Him and proclaim, *"The Lord reigns."*

Creation itself joins the song: *"Let the heavens rejoice, let the earth be glad; let the sea resound... let the fields be jubilant."* Even the trees sing for joy as the Lord comes to judge the earth. But God's judgment is not feared - it's welcomed. *"He will judge the world in righteousness and the peoples in his truth."*

Key Verse: (v.1)

"Sing to the Lord a new song; sing to the Lord, all the earth."

Application:

Psalm 96 reminds us that worship is global and joyful. Our God is not a tribal deity - He is the Maker and Judge of all. Let your worship proclaim His glory. Share His goodness with others and live in a way that honours His reign. The whole world is invited - will you respond?

PSALM 97

Author: Unknown

Theme: The Lord reigns in righteousness and glory.

Summary:

Psalm 97 opens with bold affirmation: *"The Lord reigns, let the earth be glad; let the distant shores rejoice."* This is a cosmic declaration of God's sovereign rule, extending joy even to the most remote parts of the world.

God's presence is described in awe-inspiring terms: *"Clouds and thick darkness surround him; righteousness and justice are the foundation of his throne."* His reign is holy, mysterious, and morally grounded. Fire goes before Him, lightning illuminates the world, and the earth trembles - God's power is fearsome and undeniable.

The Psalm asserts that all false worship will be shamed: *"All who worship images are put to shame… worship him, all you gods!"* Zion rejoices because the Lord's justice exalts her above other lands.

The righteous are encouraged: *"Light shines on the righteous and joy on the upright in heart."* God's rule brings not only fear to the wicked but blessing and illumination to the faithful. The final verse is a charge: *"Rejoice in the Lord, you who are righteous, and praise his holy name."* This Psalm balances the majesty of God's justice with the joy of His faithful people.

Key Verse: (v.1)

"The Lord reigns, let the earth be glad; let the distant shores rejoice."

Application:

Psalm 97 invites you to live in the light of God's rule. His throne is built on righteousness and justice - so let those qualities shape your life. Reject false idols, celebrate His supremacy, and let joy and reverence fill your heart. The King is on the throne - rejoice and follow Him.

PSALM 98

Author: Unknown

Theme: A song of praise for God's salvation and justice.

Summary:

Psalm 98 is a celebration of God's salvation and a call to joyful worship. *"Sing to the Lord a new song, for he has done marvellous things."* The Psalmist points to God's saving power as the reason for fresh praise. God's right hand and holy arm *"have worked salvation for him."* This salvation is not private - it is public and universal: *"The Lord has made his salvation known and revealed his righteousness to the nations."*

The theme of covenant faithfulness appears again: *"He has remembered his love and his faithfulness to Israel."* Yet this faithfulness benefits the whole world: *"All the ends of the earth have seen the salvation of our God."*

The Psalm moves from proclamation to exuberant praise: *"Shout for joy to the Lord, all the earth... burst into jubilant song with music."* Worship includes instruments - lyres, trumpets, and horns - as the people exalt their King. Even nature joins in: *"Let the sea resound... the world and all who live in it... let the rivers clap their hands."* The Psalm builds to a vision of creation rejoicing as God comes *"to judge the earth."*

This judgment is not to be feared by the faithful: *"He will judge the world in righteousness and the peoples with equity."* God's justice is reason for celebration.

Key Verse: (v.3)

"All the ends of the earth have seen the salvation of our God."

Application:

Psalm 98 calls us to worship with joy and boldness. God's salvation is not a secret - it's a global announcement. Praise Him with your voice, your life, and your joy. Let the world see through you that the Lord is King, and His righteousness is good news for all.

PSALM 99

Author: Unknown

Theme: The holiness and justice of God the King.

Summary:

Psalm 99 declares the absolute holiness of God and calls people to worship with reverence. It opens: *"The Lord reigns, let the nations tremble; he sits enthroned between the cherubim, let the earth shake."*

This places God at the very heart of sacred space - on His heavenly throne. *"The Lord is great in Zion; he is exalted over all the nations."* God's greatness is not limited to one people - He is supreme over all. The refrain *"He is holy"* appears three times, underscoring the theme of divine holiness.

"Exalt the Lord our God and worship at his footstool; he is holy." Holiness is not only awe-inspiring - it invites a response. We are to bow low before the King who is pure and righteous.

The Psalm also honours God's just rule: *"The King is mighty, he loves justice... in Jacob you have done what is just and right."* Historical figures are mentioned: *"Moses and Aaron... and Samuel were among his priests."* They called on the Lord, and He answered. Though He disciplined Israel, He forgave them.

The Psalm ends: *"Exalt the Lord our God and worship at his holy mountain, for the Lord our God is holy."* It's a call to worship rooted in reverence, memory, and truth.

Key Verse: (v.9)
"Exalt the Lord our God and worship at his holy mountain, for the Lord our God is holy."

Application:

Psalm 99 reminds us that God's holiness is both awe-inspiring and relational. He is just, He hears our prayers, and He forgives. Worship Him with humility and gratitude. Let His holiness shape your life - and draw near with reverence and joy.

PSALM 100

Author: Unknown

Theme: A call to joyful worship and thankful service.

Summary:

Psalm 100 is one of the most well-known and cherished Psalms, a concise yet profound call to joyful worship. It begins: *"Shout for joy to the Lord, all the earth."* The entire world is summoned to join in a celebration of God's goodness. *"Worship the Lord with gladness; come before him with joyful songs."* Worship is not to be cold or mechanical - it is heartfelt, vibrant, and filled with praise.

The Psalm reminds us of who God is: *"Know that the Lord is God. It is he who made us, and we are his; we are his people, the sheep of his pasture."* This truth is both theological and personal. We belong to God, and He lovingly tends to us. The invitation continues: *"Enter his gates with thanksgiving and his courts with praise."* Gratitude is the posture of a worshipper who knows God's grace.

The final verse proclaims: *"For the Lord is good and his love endures forever; his faithfulness continues through all generations."* These truths are the foundation for lasting praise - God's goodness, love, and faithfulness never end. Psalm 100 bridges doctrine and devotion. God's attributes - His goodness, enduring love, and generational faithfulness - form the backbone of lasting worship. When we reflect on who He is and what He has done, gratitude becomes natural and joy overflows.

Key Verse: (v.4)

"Enter his gates with thanksgiving and his courts with praise; give thanks to him and praise his name."

Application:

Psalm 100 calls us to live lives of joyful gratitude. Worship is our response to the God who made us, loves us, and is forever faithful. Don't reserve praise for perfect days - bring your thanksgiving every day. God is good, and He is worthy of your joyful worship.

PSALM 101

Author: David

Theme: A commitment to righteous leadership.

Summary:

Psalm 101 is David's personal pledge to rule with integrity and godliness. It begins: *"I will sing of your love and justice; to you, Lord, I will sing praise."*

David then turns inward: *"I will be careful to lead a blameless life - when will you come to me?"* He is not merely making a public declaration but seeking to align his private life with God's standards. His desire to live *"within my house with a blameless heart"* shows that righteousness begins at home.

He rejects wickedness and moral compromise: *"I will not look with approval on anything that is vile ... no one who practices deceit will dwell in my house."* Instead, David will surround himself with the faithful: *"My eyes will be on the faithful in the land, that they may dwell with me."* This isn't just about leadership style - it reflects God's own priorities. Leaders in the kingdom are called to uphold truth, honour, and justice.

The Psalm ends with a firm resolve: *"Every morning I will put to silence all the wicked in the land."* This rhythm of accountability suggests that maintaining righteousness is a constant task requiring vigilance and resolve.

Key Verse: (v.2)

"I will be careful to lead a blameless life - when will you come to me?"

Application:

Psalm 101 challenges anyone in leadership to pursue integrity. Whether you lead a nation, a workplace, a ministry, or a home, God calls you to live blamelessly. Surround yourself with people of integrity, reject corruption, and begin by being faithful in your own house. Leadership begins with personal holiness.

PSALM 102

Author: **Unknown**

Theme: A prayer in affliction and a declaration of God's eternal reign.

Summary:

Psalm 102 begins with a desperate cry: *"Hear my prayer, Lord; let my cry for help come to you."* It is the lament of a person overwhelmed by sorrow, weakened in body, and distressed in spirit. *"My days vanish like smoke… my bones burn like glowing embers."* The language is raw and deeply human. The Psalmist feels isolated and forgotten: *"I lie awake; I have become like a bird alone on a roof."* His suffering has made him feel like a shadow, fading and insubstantial. Yet in spite of affliction, his focus turns to the unchanging nature of God. *"But you, Lord, sit enthroned forever; your renown endures through all generations."* The contrast is stark - while the Psalmist's life fades, God remains eternal.

The Psalm moves from personal lament to prophetic hope. Nations will fear God's name, and the Lord *"will rebuild Zion and appear in his glory."* Even those yet unborn will hear of God's deliverance: *"Let this be written for a future generation."* The final section rejoices in God's unchanging nature: *"In the beginning you laid the foundations of the earth… but you remain the same, and your years will never end."* This offers profound comfort - the Psalmist's frailty is anchored in God's strength.

Key Verse: (v.12)

"But you, Lord, sit enthroned forever; your renown endures through all generations."

Application:

Psalm 102 speaks to anyone facing deep suffering. Though our lives are fleeting, God is unchanging. He hears, He restores, and He acts for the good of His people. When pain clouds your view, fix your eyes on God's eternal throne. He remains faithful through every generation.

PSALM 103

Author: David

Theme: Blessing the Lord for His mercy and compassion.

Summary:

Psalm 103 is a rich, poetic celebration of God's mercy and compassion. David begins with a personal call to worship: *"Praise the Lord, my soul; all my inmost being, praise his holy name."* It's not enough to give lip service - worship must rise from deep within. He lists reasons to bless the Lord: *"who forgives all your sins and heals all your diseases, who redeems your life from the pit."* God is not only a healer and redeemer - He *"crowns you with love and compassion."* His benefits are personal and comprehensive.

David then reflects more on God's righteousness: *"The Lord works righteousness and justice for all the oppressed."* He remembers God's mercy to Moses and Israel, reminding us that, *"The Lord is compassionate and gracious, slow to anger, abounding in love."* God's mercy is immense: *"He does not treat us as our sins deserve."* Instead, *"as far as the east is from the west, so far has he removed our transgressions from us."*

David contrasts our frailty with God's permanence: *"The life of mortals is like grass... but from everlasting to everlasting the Lord's love is with those who fear him."* God's love outlasts generations. The Psalm closes with a cosmic invitation: *"Praise the Lord, you his angels... you his heavenly hosts... all his works everywhere in his dominion."* It ends where it began - with a call to personal praise.

Key Verse: (v.12)
"As far as the east is from the west, so far has he removed our transgressions from us."

Application:

Psalm 103 invites you to reflect deeply on God's mercy. No matter your past, God's love reaches further. Let His forgiveness move you to praise - not just with your lips, but with your whole being. Remember His benefits and bless His name daily.

PSALM 104

Author: Unknown

Theme: Celebrating God as Creator and Sustainer.

Summary:

Psalm 104 is a sweeping hymn that celebrates God's work in creation. It begins with wonder: *"Praise the Lord, my soul. Lord my God, you are very great."* The Psalmist pictures God *"wrapped in light as with a garment,"* riding the clouds and making winds His messengers. He describes the stability of the earth: *"You set the earth on its foundations... covered it with the watery depths."* God's voice rebukes the waters, setting boundaries they cannot cross.

The Psalmist delights in the order of creation: springs water the fields; birds nest beside streams; the earth is satisfied with God's provision. He speaks of wine, oil, and bread as gifts from God that gladden, nourish, and sustain life. God provides not only for humans but also animals: *"The lions roar for their prey and seek their food from God."* Day and night serve different purposes.

The Psalmist marvels at God's control: *"When you hide your face, they are terrified... when you send your Spirit, they are created."* Life and death are in His hands. The song ends with praise: *"May the glory of the Lord endure forever... I will sing to the Lord all my life."* Even the sinner is addressed - *"may sinners vanish from the earth"* - not out of spite, but from longing for a world fully restored.

Key Verse: (v.30)

"When you send your Spirit, they are created, and you renew the face of the ground."

Application:

Psalm 104 invites us to see the world as God's ongoing masterpiece. Nature is not random - it is designed, loved, and sustained. Join in the praise of creation. Recognize God's hand in every sunrise, every meal, and every breath. He is worthy of lifelong worship.

PSALM 105

Author: Unknown
Theme: Remembering God's faithfulness through history.

Summary:
Psalm 105 is a historical Psalm that traces God's faithfulness to His covenant people. It opens with an invitation: *"Give praise to the Lord, proclaim his name; make known among the nations what he has done."* Gratitude leads to witness. The Psalm celebrates God's works: *"Sing to him… tell of all his wonderful acts."* God's wonders are not forgotten. His covenant with Abraham is remembered, as is His promise to Isaac and confirmation to Jacob.

The Psalm recounts how God protected His people: *"He allowed no one to oppress them; for their sake he rebuked kings."* Even famine was part of His plan - He sent Joseph ahead into Egypt. God's control over history is emphasized: from Joseph's rise to power, to Israel's multiplication in Egypt, to Moses' deliverance. Plagues are described as divine acts - not random disasters, but purposeful interventions.

The Exodus is celebrated: *"He brought out Israel, laden with silver and gold… the Lord spread a cloud for a covering and fire to give light at night."* God provided manna, quail, and water from a rock. The Psalm ends: *"For he remembered his holy promise… he brought out his people with rejoicing."* God's acts were all in fulfillment of covenant promises.

Key Verse: (v.5)
"Remember the wonders he has done, his miracles, and the judgments he pronounced."

Application:
Psalm 105 reminds us to remember. God's faithfulness stretches across generations. Rehearse His goodness in your own life and proclaim it to others. Gratitude fuels faith, and memory strengthens obedience. Never forget what He has done.

PSALM 106

Author: Unknown

Theme: Confession and praise for God's enduring mercy.

Summary:

Psalm 106 is a companion to Psalm 105, but it presents the darker side of Israel's history - one of rebellion, forgetfulness, and sin. It begins with a declaration of God's goodness: *"Praise the Lord. Give thanks to the Lord, for he is good; his love endures forever."*

The Psalmist quickly moves to confession: *"We have sinned, even as our ancestors did; we have done wrong and acted wickedly."* He recounts how Israel rebelled at the Red Sea, forgetting God's miraculous deliverance from Egypt. Despite their disobedience, *"he saved them for his name's sake, to make his mighty power known."*

The pattern continues: God shows mercy, Israel rebels, God disciplines, and then forgives. The Psalmist does not gloss over the consequences. Many died due to their disobedience. Yet God's covenant love endured. *"Many times he delivered them, but they were bent on rebellion."* Still, *"he took note of their distress when he heard their cry."*

The Psalm concludes with a prayer for restoration: *"Save us, Lord our God, and gather us from the nations, that we may give thanks to your holy name."*

Key Verse: (v.8)
"But he saved them for his name's sake, to make his mighty power known."

Application:

Psalm 106 is a mirror for all of us. Though we may forget, fall, and rebel, God's mercy endures forever. This Psalm calls us to remember, repent, and return. Like Israel, we too need saving grace - not once, but daily. Let this history stir humility and deep gratitude in all of us, as we praise the God who never gives up on His people.

PSALM 107

Author: Unknown

Theme: Gratitude for God's deliverance in various trials.

Summary:

Psalm 107 is a vibrant and diverse hymn of thanksgiving, structured around four types of people who were in distress and whom God rescued. It opens with the familiar invitation: *"Give thanks to the Lord, for he is good; his love endures forever."* The redeemed are called to speak out about their deliverance - proof of God's mercy in action. First, it describes those wandering in the wilderness, homeless and hungry. *"They cried out to the Lord in their trouble, and he delivered them from their distress."* Next, it recounts those imprisoned in darkness for rebelling against God's words, yet who also cried out and were saved. The third group are those suffering physical affliction due to sin.

Finally, the Psalm tells of sailors caught in a terrifying storm. When they cried out, God stilled the storm and brought them safely to harbour. Each scenario follows a similar pattern: distress, cry for help, divine intervention, and a call to give thanks. Four times, the refrain is repeated: *"Let them give thanks to the Lord for his unfailing love and his wonderful deeds for mankind."* The final verses shift to broader reflections on God's rule in the world. He humbles the proud, lifts the needy, and blesses the righteous. The Psalm concludes: "Let the one who is wise heed these things and ponder the loving deeds of the Lord."

Key Verse: (v.8)

"Let them give thanks to the Lord for his unfailing love and his wonderful deeds for mankind."

Application:

Psalm 107 teaches that God meets us in every type of crisis. Whether we are lost, imprisoned, sick, or terrified, His mercy is near. Our task is to cry out to Him and to give thanks when He answers. Reflect often on how God has helped you and be quick to share your testimony.

PSALM 108

Author: David

Theme: A confident plea for God's help.

Summary:

Psalm 108 is a beautiful blend of confident praise and bold petition. David begins with determination: *"My heart, O God, is steadfast; I will sing and make music with all my soul."*

His worship is wholehearted and intentional. Even before the day dawns, David is ready to praise: *"I will awaken the dawn."* His vision is expansive: *"I will praise you, Lord, among the nations."* This is not private worship but a global declaration of God's steadfast love and faithfulness.

The Psalm then turns to prayer: *"Save us and help us with your right hand, that those you love may be delivered."* This is not a cry of desperation but a confident appeal grounded in God's covenant love. David recognizes that victory does not lie in human strength: *"Give us aid against the enemy, for human help is worthless."* This is a vital declaration of faith. Without God, success is impossible - but with God, victory is assured.

The Psalm closes triumphantly: *"With God we will gain the victory, and he will trample down our enemies."* This is not arrogance, but assurance rooted in God's power and promise.

Key Verse: (vv.12-13)

"Give us aid against the enemy, for human help is worthless. With God we will gain the victory."

Application:

Psalm 108 encourages us to worship with confidence and pray with boldness. As David shows, praise is a prelude to victory. When we remember who God is and what He has promised, we can face every challenge with courage. Don't depend on your own strength - trust in God's faithfulness.

PSALM 109

Author: David

Theme: A cry for justice and vindication amid betrayal.

Summary:

Psalm 109 begins with a plea: *"My God, whom I praise, do not remain silent."* David is under vicious verbal attack. He describes how wicked and deceitful people have spoken against him with lying tongues. Despite his love, they repay him with accusations. *"In return for my friendship they accuse me, but I am a man of prayer."* What follows is a striking curse, calling for God's judgment on his enemies. These verses can be shocking to modern readers, but they reflect the deep pain and sense of injustice David feels.

The tone shifts in verse 21. David returns to a plea for mercy: *"But you, Sovereign Lord, help me for your name's sake; out of the goodness of your love, deliver me."* David then acknowledges his vulnerability. *"I am poor and needy, and my heart is wounded within me."* The Psalm becomes deeply personal. David knows that his deliverance will serve a higher purpose: *"Let them know that it is your hand, that you, Lord, have done it."* His vindication is not merely personal - it is a testimony to God's justice and power. The Psalm ends with a vow to praise: "With my mouth I will greatly extol the Lord… for he stands *at the right hand of the needy, to save their lives from those who would condemn them."*

Key Verse: (v.21)
"But you, Sovereign Lord, help me for your name's sake; out of the goodness of your love, deliver me."

Application:

Psalm 109 reminds us that we can bring even our darkest emotions to God. When we feel betrayed, falsely accused, or wounded, we don't have to suppress our pain. We can cry out for justice, knowing that God hears and acts righteously. God welcomes the prayers of the broken-hearted. In the end, trust wins out - God defends and restores His people.

PSALM 110

Author: David

Theme: The reign of the Messiah as eternal King and Priest.

Summary:

Psalm 110 is a deeply significant messianic Psalm, the most quoted Old Testament passage in the New Testament. Jesus Himself refers to it in Matthew 22:44 to reveal His divine nature. The Psalm opens with a divine declaration: *"The Lord says to my Lord: 'Sit at my right hand until I make your enemies a footstool for your feet.'"* Here, David describes a conversation between God the Father ("The Lord") and the Messiah ("my Lord"), affirming the Messiah's authority and eternal rule.

Verse 4 introduces a radical concept: *"You are a priest forever, in the order of Melchizedek."* This is extraordinary because it blends two roles that were otherwise separate in Israel - king and priest. Melchizedek, the mysterious priest-king of Salem mentioned in Genesis 14, becomes a prototype for Christ. This verse underpins much of the theology in the New Testament book of Hebrews.

The final verses of the Psalm describe a warrior-king executing justice: *"The Lord is at your right hand; he will crush kings on the day of his wrath."* The Messiah's reign is righteous and decisive. *"He will judge the nations… he will drink from a brook along the way, and so he will lift his head high."* This image reflects both the intensity and the refreshment of His victorious mission.

Key Verse: (v.4)

"You are a priest forever, in the order of Melchizedek."

Application:

Psalm 110 calls us to bow in reverence before Jesus, our eternal King and Priest. In a world filled with temporary rulers and broken systems, we are reminded that Jesus reigns supreme. His throne is unshakable, His priesthood is unending, and His justice is perfect. Trust in His rule, rely on His intercession, and live with confidence under His lordship.

PSALM 111

Author: Unknown

Theme: Praise for God's glorious works.

Summary:

Psalm 111 is a concise yet powerful celebration of the character and works of the Lord. Structured as an acrostic in Hebrew (each line beginning with a successive letter of the alphabet), it opens with a call to wholehearted praise: *"I will extol the Lord with all my heart in the council of the upright and in the assembly."* Worship here is both personal and public.

The Psalmist highlights the greatness of God's works: *"Great are the works of the Lord; they are pondered by all who delight in them."* These works are not fleeting or shallow - they are *"glorious and majestic,"* and they reveal His righteousness, which *"endures forever."*

A key aspect of Psalm 111 is its focus on God's provision and faithfulness: *"He provides food for those who fear him; he remembers his covenant forever."* This echoes God's care for Israel in the wilderness and reassures the faithful of His ongoing provision. The Psalmist then shifts to redemption: *"He provided redemption for his people; he ordained his covenant forever - holy and awesome is his name."* The Psalm ends with wisdom: *"The fear of the Lord is the beginning of wisdom; all who follow his precepts have good understanding."* True knowledge begins with reverence for God.

Key Verse: (v.10)
"The fear of the Lord is the beginning of wisdom; all who follow his precepts have good understanding."

Application:

Psalm 111 encourages us to slow down and consider the greatness of God's works. Reflect on His provision, study His Word, and respond with reverent obedience. Worship is not based on emotion alone - it grows as we ponder God's glory and stand in awe of His enduring righteousness.

PSALM 112

Author: Unknown

Theme: The blessings of those who fear the Lord.

Summary:

Psalm 112 serves as a counterpart to Psalm 111. While Psalm 111 praises the works and character of God, this Psalm reflects on the character and blessings of the person who fears the Lord. It begins with an enthusiastic call: *"Praise the Lord. Blessed are those who fear the Lord, who find great delight in his commands."* The Psalm outlines blessings that flow from fearing the Lord. First is legacy: *"Their children will be mighty in the land; the generation of the upright will be blessed."* The godly life has a flow on effect, influencing future generations. Material blessing is also noted: *"Wealth and riches are in their houses, and their righteousness endures forever."*

Light and hope characterize this person: *"Even in darkness light dawns for the upright, for those who are gracious and compassionate and righteous."* The Psalm highlights inner virtues such as generosity, justice, and courage. *"Good will come to those who are generous and lend freely, who conduct their affairs with justice."* God blesses those who reflect His character. The righteous person is not shaken by bad news. *"Surely the righteous will never be shaken… They will have no fear of bad news; their hearts are steadfast, trusting in the Lord."* This calm assurance in the face of life's uncertainties sets the godly apart. The Psalm concludes by contrasting the fate of the wicked: *"The wicked will see and be vexed, they will gnash their teeth and waste away."*

Key Verse: (v.7)

"They will have no fear of bad news; their hearts are steadfast, trusting in the Lord."

Application:

Psalm 112 paints a portrait of the fruitful, faithful life. This Psalm invites us to pursue character over comfort and integrity over instant reward. When our hearts are anchored in God, we can face any situation with confidence.

PSALM 113

Author: Unknown

Theme: God's majesty and mercy.

Summary:

Psalm 113 begins and ends with the same call: *"Praise the Lord."* It is the first of the Hallel Psalms (Psalms 113–118), traditionally sung during Jewish festivals like Passover. This Psalm focuses on the greatness of God and His gracious attention to the lowly. The opening verses set the tone of celebration: *"Praise, O servants of the Lord, praise the name of the Lord."* God's name is exalted from dawn to dusk, *"from the rising of the sun to the place where it sets."* His glory fills the earth, and His name is continually honoured.

The Psalm then shifts to God's exalted position: *"The Lord is exalted over all the nations, his glory above the heavens."* No one is like our God, who dwells on high yet stoops down to look on the heavens and the earth. This contrast is striking - God is both infinitely majestic and intimately involved with His creation.

Then comes a stunning portrait of grace. *"He raises the poor from the dust and lifts the needy from the ash heap."* God exalts the lowly, seats them with princes, and transforms their circumstances. This is not only a reflection of His power but of His compassion. The final verse speaks of personal restoration: *"He settles the childless woman in her home as a happy mother of children."* God brings joy and dignity to the forgotten and the barren.

Key Verse: (v.7)

"He raises the poor from the dust and lifts the needy from the ash heap."

Application:

Psalm 113 reminds us that the God who rules the universe also lifts the broken-hearted. He is not distant or indifferent - He stoops to restore, to bless, and to heal. Let this truth move you to heartfelt praise, especially when life feels low. No one is too small for His notice or too forgotten for His mercy.

PSALM 114

Author: Unknown

Theme: The earth trembles at God's presence.

Summary:

Psalm 114 is a poetic celebration of God's mighty acts during Israel's Exodus from Egypt. The Psalm opens by describing the moment of national transformation: *"When Israel came out of Egypt, Jacob from a people of foreign tongue."* This marked the beginning of Israel's identity as God's covenant people. It then states, *"Judah became God's sanctuary, Israel his dominion."*

The Psalm then turns to dramatic imagery from nature: *"The sea looked and fled, the Jordan turned back."* These lines refer to the parting of the Red Sea and the Jordan River, key miracles during Israel's journey. Nature itself recognizes the power and presence of the Lord. The mountains *"leaped like rams, the hills like lambs,"* possibly a poetic description of Mount Sinai quaking. The Psalmist then asks mockingly rhetorical questions: *"Why was it, sea, that you fled?"* The obvious answer is: because the Creator of the universe was present.

The Psalm closes with a command: *"Tremble, earth, at the presence of the Lord, at the presence of the God of Jacob, who turned the rock into a pool, the hard rock into springs of water."* The God who shakes the mountains also provides for His people.

Key Verse: (vv.7-8)
"Tremble, earth, at the presence of the Lord… who turned the rock into a pool."

Application:

Psalm 114 reminds us that God's presence brings transformation. Obstacles become highways, deserts become fountains, and the natural order yields to the supernatural. If creation trembles before God, how much more should we revere Him? And yet, the same God who causes the mountains to quake also quenches our thirst in dry places. Worship Him with awe - and with trust.

PSALM 115

Author: Unknown

Theme: The folly of idols and the faithfulness of God.

Summary:

Psalm 115 contrasts the living, active God of Israel with the lifeless idols of the nations. It begins with a declaration of humility and purpose: *"Not to us, Lord, not to us but to your name be the glory, because of your love and faithfulness."* God's people give Him glory not for their achievements but because of who He is. The Psalm then responds to a challenge from the nations: *"Where is their God?"* The reply is bold: *"Our God is in heaven; he does whatever pleases him."* This affirms God's sovereignty.

In contrast, the Psalm ridicules idols: *"But their idols are silver and gold, made by human hands. They have mouths, but cannot speak, eyes, but cannot see..."* Worshiping false gods ultimately dehumanizes and blinds the worshipper. Verses 9–11 form a repeated call: *"All you Israelites... house of Aaron... you who fear him - trust in the Lord! He is their help and shield."* This call to trust acknowledges that God protects and provides for His people. The Psalm then speaks of blessing: *"The Lord remembers us and will bless us... he will bless those who fear the Lord - small and great alike."* God's blessings are not selective. They are generous and inclusive.

The final verses emphasize God's dominion: *"The highest heavens belong to the Lord, but the earth he has given to mankind ... it is we who extol the Lord, both now and forevermore."*

Key Verse: (v.3)
"Our God is in heaven; he does whatever pleases him."

Application:

Psalm 115 challenges us to trust in the living God instead of lifeless substitutes. Anything we exalt above God becomes an idol - even if it's a good thing. But idols cannot save, speak, or respond. Only God can bless, protect, and lead. Give glory to Him alone and place your trust in His faithful hands.

PSALM 116

Author: Unknown

Theme: Gratitude for answered prayer.

Summary:

Psalm 116 is a deeply personal Psalm of thanksgiving. It begins with heartfelt emotion: *"I love the Lord, for he heard my voice; he heard my cry for mercy."* The Psalmist recalls a moment of desperate need: *"The cords of death entangled me... I was overcome by distress and sorrow."* But when he called on the Lord, he experienced deliverance. He then reflects on God's nature: *"The Lord is gracious and righteous; our God is full of compassion."* This is a theological anchor in times of trial. The writer continues, *"When I was brought low, he saved me."* The rescue is described with gratitude and relief. *"You, Lord, have delivered me from death, my eyes from tears, my feet from stumbling."* Now the Psalmist walks with God *"in the land of the living."*

In response, he asks: *"What shall I return to the Lord for all his goodness to me?"* The answer: a life of worship and public testimony. *"I will fulfill my vows to the Lord in the presence of all his people."* He drinks the *"cup of salvation"* and praises God openly. A beloved verse appears near the end: *"Precious in the sight of the Lord is the death of his faithful servants."* God sees, values, and honours His people even in their final moments.

Key Verse: (v.1)

"I love the Lord, for he heard my voice; he heard my cry for mercy."

Application:

Psalm 116 reminds us to look back with gratitude on the times God has rescued us. There are many. Every answered prayer deserves a testimony. Like the Psalmist, we should commit to public praise and wholehearted obedience. God not only hears, He saves - and that is reason enough to love Him deeply and praise Him daily.

PSALM 117

Author: Unknown

Theme: A global call to praise the Lord.

Summary:

Psalm 117, though the shortest chapter in the Bible, carries an expansive and profound message. In just two short verses, the Psalmist summons the entire world to join in praising the Lord: *"Praise the Lord, all you nations; extol him, all you peoples."* Every tribe, every nation, and every people are commanded to give glory to the God of heaven. What makes this Psalm especially remarkable is its prophetic nature. Long before the gospel was preached to the Gentiles, Psalm 117 anticipates a time when all peoples would come to worship the one true God.

The Psalm provides two reasons for this call to praise: *"For great is his love toward us, and the faithfulness of the Lord endures forever."* The love referred to here is God's covenant love - steadfast, loyal, and gracious. It is not earned but freely given. The word *"faithfulness"* reflects God's reliability, consistency, and truth.

Though brief, the Psalm offers a rich theology of worship. God's love and faithfulness are not limited by geography, culture, or ethnicity. He is not a tribal deity but the Creator and Redeemer of all. And because His love is *"great"* and His faithfulness *"endures forever,"* our praise should be as wide-reaching and as unending as His attributes. The Psalm ends, fittingly, with a powerful affirmation: *"Praise the Lord."*

Key Verse: (v.1)

"Praise the Lord, all you nations; extol him, all you peoples."

Application:

Psalm 117 reminds us that worship belongs to all people. It challenges us to lift our eyes beyond ourselves and see God's heart for the nations. As recipients of His enduring love and faithfulness, we are to lead the global chorus of praise and invite others into it. God is not just our God - He is the God of all.

PSALM 118

Author: Unknown

Theme: Victory and thanksgiving through God's steadfast love.

Summary:

Psalm 118 is a joyful and triumphant Psalm of thanksgiving, often associated with public worship during festivals. It begins and ends with the same resounding declaration: *"Give thanks to the Lord, for he is good; his love endures forever."* This refrain, repeated throughout the Psalm, anchors the entire message in the unshakable love of God.

The Psalmist recounts a personal and national experience of being surrounded by enemies and delivered by God's power. *"When hard pressed, I cried to the Lord; he brought me into a spacious place."* The imagery is one of divine rescue from oppression into freedom. This is a Psalm of someone who has experienced God's help firsthand.

A repeated theme is trust: *"The Lord is with me; I will not be afraid. What can mere mortals do to me?"* The writer urges others to place their confidence not in princes or human strength, but in the Lord alone. God has become the Psalmist's strength, song, and salvation. One of the most quoted verses in the New Testament is found here: *"The stone the builders rejected has become the cornerstone."* (v.22) Jesus applied this verse to Himself (Matthew 21:42), revealing that He is the foundation of God's redemptive plan - even though He was initially rejected.

Key Verse: (vv. 1 & 29)
"Give thanks to the Lord, for he is good; his love endures forever."

Application:

Psalm 118 reminds us that God is both our defender and our foundation. In every moment of trial or triumph, His love does not waver. Like the Psalmist, we are called to trust Him, praise Him, and build our lives on the cornerstone - Jesus Christ.

PSALM 119

Author: Traditionally attributed to David

Theme: Loving, living, and learning the Word of God.

Summary:

Psalm 119 is the longest chapter in the Bible, composed of 176 verses arranged as an acrostic spanning across 22 stanzas, each corresponding to a letter of the Hebrew alphabet. Every verse refers to the Word of God - using terms such as "law," "statutes," "precepts," "commands," "decrees," and "promises." Despite its length, the message is simple and profound: God's Word is essential for life.

The Psalm opens with a declaration of blessing for those *"whose ways are blameless, who walk according to the law of the Lord."* The Psalmist sees Scripture not as a burden, but as a path to joy, purity, and purpose. It shapes the heart and guides the steps: *"Your word is a lamp for my feet, a light on my path."* The Psalmist acknowledges trials, persecution, and sorrow, but consistently returns to the comfort and strength found in Scripture. *"Trouble and distress have come upon me, but your commands give me delight."* Even in affliction, God's Word is a sustaining force.

In many ways, this Psalm reflects the full journey of faith: struggle, hope, joy, failure, renewal, and dependence. All of it is shaped and sustained by a devotion to God's Word. The repetition never grows weary - it deepens the impact, like waves reinforcing a shoreline.

Key Verse: (v.105)

"Your word is a lamp for my feet, a light on my path."

Application:

Psalm 119 challenges us to treasure Scripture - not as a book of rules, but as a living guide that reveals God's heart. If you long for clarity, peace, and strength, immerse yourself in the Word. Pray it, obey it, and delight in it. Let God's truth light your path, especially when the road is uncertain or dark.

PSALM 120

Author: Unknown

Theme: A cry for peace in a hostile world.

Summary:

Psalm 120 marks the beginning of the *"Songs of Ascents,"* a collection of Psalms (120–134) traditionally sung by pilgrims journeying to Jerusalem. The Psalmist is in a place of tension, surrounded by lies and conflict, and longs for peace. *"I call on the Lord in my distress, and he answers me."* The journey toward God starts where many spiritual journeys begin - in pain and frustration. The problem is clearly stated: deception. *"Save me, Lord, from lying lips and from deceitful tongues."*

This Psalm is not only about deceitful speech - it's about exile. The Psalmist laments, *"Woe to me that I dwell in Meshek, that I live among the tents of Kedar!"* These distant, hostile places represent spiritual and cultural dislocation. The writer feels alienated and out of place, longing for the peace of Jerusalem and the fellowship of God's people.

The pain is not only physical or geographic - it is relational and emotional: *"I am for peace; but when I speak, they are for war."* The Psalmist desires peace, but those around him seek strife. It is a cry of frustration that resonates with anyone who has ever tried to live righteously in a world set on conflict.

Key Verse: (v.7)

"I am for peace; but when I speak, they are for war."

Application:

Psalm 120 reminds us that our journey toward God often begins in discomfort. We don't always begin our walk with joy - we begin with longing. Surrounded by falsehood and hostility, we cry out to the Lord, and He hears. When you feel like a stranger in a foreign land, remember that you are not alone. Let your frustration drive you toward God's presence, not away from it. The road to peace begins with prayer.

PSALM 121

Author: Unknown

Theme: God is our constant help and protector.

Summary:
Psalm 121 is a beloved Psalm of assurance, often recited by those seeking comfort in uncertain times. It begins with a searching question: *"I lift up my eyes to the mountains – where does my help come from?"* In ancient times, the mountains could represent both danger and false worship, but also strength and security. The answer is immediately given: *"My help comes from the Lord, the Maker of heaven and earth."* Help doesn't come from creation, but from the Creator.

The Psalm unfolds as a declaration of God's ongoing care. *"He will not let your foot slip - he who watches over you will not slumber."* God is never inattentive or unaware.

The repetition of the phrase *"watches over you"* emphasizes God's role as a vigilant guardian. He is described as *"your shade at your right hand,"* meaning He is close, protective, and always present. Neither the scorching sun nor the mysterious moon will harm you, symbolizing round-the-clock divine protection.

The final verses assure us of God's comprehensive care: *"The Lord will keep you from all harm - he will watch over your life."* His protection extends to every part of our journey, both now and forevermore.

Key Verse: (v.2)
"My help comes from the Lord, the Maker of heaven and earth."

Application:
Psalm 121 reminds us that God is not distant or dormant. He is our ever-present help, our shield, and our sustainer. When life feels uncertain or threatening, lift your eyes not to the hills but to the One who made them. Trust the Lord who never sleeps and never steps away from His people.

PSALM 122

Author: David

Theme: Joy in worship and peace in the city of God.

Summary:

Psalm 122 is a joyful reflection on the privilege of worship and the beauty of Jerusalem. *"I rejoiced with those who said to me, 'Let us go to the house of the Lord.'"* This is the voice of a pilgrim arriving in Jerusalem for one of the great feasts. The journey is complete, and the destination is not only a physical place, but a spiritual home. Jerusalem is described in glowing terms: *"Built like a city that is closely compacted together."* Its structure symbolizes unity and strength. It is also the seat of justice and divine appointment: *"There the thrones for judgment stand, the thrones of the house of David."* This is not only a civic centre but a place where God's rule is acknowledged.

The Psalmist then calls the people to pray for the peace of Jerusalem. *"Pray for the peace of Jerusalem: 'May those who love you be secure.'"* This is both a prayer and a blessing - for the city, for worshippers, and for the future of God's people. Peace ("shalom") and security are recurring themes, pointing to the deeper wholeness God intends for His people.

David makes it personal: *"For the sake of my family and friends, I will say, 'Peace be within you.'"* Love for the city of God reflects love for God's people.

Key Verse: (v.1)

"I rejoiced with those who said to me, 'Let us go to the house of the Lord.'"

Application:

Psalm 122 reminds us to celebrate and prioritize gathered worship. Just as ancient Israel journeyed with joy to meet with God, so should we. It also challenges us to pray for the peace and unity of God's people. The church is our spiritual Jerusalem - let's approach it with joy and pray for its peace.

PSALM 123

Author: Unknown

Theme: Humble dependence on God's mercy.

Summary:

Psalm 123 is a short yet deeply reverent cry for mercy. *"I lift up my eyes to you, to you who sit enthroned in heaven."* This upward gaze expresses both trust and surrender. God is exalted above all, and yet His people look to Him with the expectancy of servants watching their master.

The imagery is striking: *"As the eyes of slaves look to the hand of their master… so our eyes look to the Lord our God, till he shows us his mercy."* This is a posture of waiting, obedience, and hope. The Psalmist knows that God is not a distant ruler but a merciful provider.

Then comes the plea: *"Have mercy on us, Lord, have mercy on us, for we have endured no end of contempt."* The people are weary of scorn, surrounded by arrogance and opposition. The prayer is not for vengeance or power, but for mercy. This is a recognition of need, not entitlement.

The Psalm ends without resolution, echoing the experience of many who pray in waiting. Yet the direction of the gaze – upward - remains firm.

Key Verse: (v.2)

"As the eyes of slaves look to the hand of their master… so our eyes look to the Lord our God."

Application:

Psalm 123 teaches us to remain fixed on God in times of struggle. When scorn and ridicule surround us, our help is not in defence but in dependence. Lift your eyes, wait for His mercy, and remain steadfast in hope. God sees. He hears. And He responds in His perfect time.

PSALM 124

Author: David

Theme: Thanksgiving for God's deliverance.

Summary:

Psalm 124 is a stirring reflection on divine intervention. David speaks on behalf of Israel, encouraging the nation to consider what would have happened *"if the Lord had not been on our side."* It's a hypothetical of disaster, used to highlight the power of God's protection. *"Let Israel say,"* he urges - this is a communal testimony, not just an individual reflection. The danger Israel faced is described in overwhelming terms: *"they would have swallowed us alive... the flood would have engulfed us... the torrent would have swept over us."* These images evoke total destruction - being consumed, drowned, and overwhelmed by forces too great to resist. But the enemy did not succeed, and the reason is clear: the Lord intervened.

David shifts from imagining defeat to declaring deliverance. *"Praise be to the Lord, who has not let us be torn by their teeth."* God is pictured as the one who pulls His people back from the jaws of death. The Psalm ends with one of the most memorable declarations in Scripture: *"Our help is in the name of the Lord, the Maker of heaven and earth."* This line reorients Israel - and us - to the foundational truth of all security. The Creator is not distant. He is our help, our defender, and our deliverer.

Key Verse: (v.1,4)

"If the Lord had not been on our side... the flood would have engulfed us."

Application:

Psalm 124 urges us to pause and reflect on the unseen ways God has delivered us. Many times, we've been closer to disaster than we knew, and it was only God's mercy that held back the flood. Gratitude is the proper response. Look back over your life and identify the "snares" God has broken on your behalf.

PSALM 125

Author: Unknown

Theme: Trust in the Lord leads to unshakable security.

Summary:

Psalm 125 paints a picture of enduring spiritual stability. *"Those who trust in the Lord are like Mount Zion, which cannot be shaken but endures forever."* Those who trust in the Lord share in that firmness. The Psalm continues with a powerful image: *"As the mountains surround Jerusalem, so the Lord surrounds his people both now and forevermore."* His presence isn't fleeting - it is eternal.

The Psalm doesn't ignore evil. *"The sceptre of the wicked will not remain over the land allotted to the righteous."* God may allow temporary testing, but wicked rule will not last. This reassurance speaks to the heart of those enduring injustice or oppression. There is a concern for moral stability as well: *"For then the righteous might use their hands to do evil."* Extended pressure can wear down even the faithful, so God steps in to sustain and protect the hearts of His people.

The prayer that follows is brief but profound: *"Do good, Lord, to those who are good, to those who are upright in heart."* This is not about perfection, but integrity. God honours sincere faithfulness. By contrast, *"those who turn to crooked ways"* will be removed from among the righteous. The final benediction, *"Peace be on Israel,"* ties the whole Psalm together. God's protection leads to peace.

Key Verse: (v.2)

"As the mountains surround Jerusalem, so the Lord surrounds his people both now and forevermore."

Application:

Psalm 125 encourages us to remain steadfast in trust. The world may shift, opposition may rise, and pressure may weigh heavily - but God surrounds His people like a mountain fortress. When life feels unstable, plant your feet in the unshakable promises of God. His presence is not momentary - it's forever.

PSALM 126

Author: Unknown

Theme: Joy in restoration and hope in future renewal.

Summary:

Psalm 126 is a song of celebration and anticipation. It reflects on a past moment when the Lord restored Israel's fortunes - possibly referring to the return from Babylonian exile. *"When the Lord restored the fortunes of Zion, we were like those who dreamed."* The joy was so profound, it felt surreal. Laughter and praise burst from the people, and even other nations took notice: *"The Lord has done great things for them."* This memory serves as both a celebration and a springboard into prayer. *"Restore our fortunes, Lord, like streams in the Negev."*

The Psalmist is asking God to do again what He has done before - to bring life and abundance where there is currently dryness and despair. The final verses use the imagery of farming to portray restoration: *"Those who sow with tears will reap with songs of joy."* The faithful may sow in seasons of sorrow, but their labour is not in vain. The one who plants weeping will one day return rejoicing, carrying sheaves of harvest.

This Psalm captures the rhythm of redemption: past joy, present longing, and future hope. It encourages believers to remember God's past goodness while continuing to trust Him in the present.

Key Verse: (v.5)

"Those who sow with tears will reap with songs of joy."

Application:

Psalm 126 encourages us to recall the goodness of God in our history as fuel for faith in our present. If He has restored before, He can restore again. Don't give up sowing righteousness, even through tears. God's promises assure us that joy is coming. Keep praying, keep planting, and expect a harvest.

PSALM 127

Author: Solomon

Theme: God's essential role in all of life.

Summary:

Psalm 127 is one of only two Psalms attributed to Solomon, and it reflects his wisdom-oriented outlook. It begins with a profound truth: *"Unless the Lord builds the house, the builders labour in vain."* Human effort, no matter how intense or skilful, is ultimately fruitless without divine blessing. This truth extends to every area of life. *"Unless the Lord watches over the city, the guards stand watch in vain."* Our attempts at safety are meaningless unless grounded in God's providence. The Psalm critiques anxious toil: *"In vain you rise early and stay up late, toiling for food to eat - for he grants sleep to those he loves."* God offers rest, not restlessness, to those who trust Him.

The second half of the Psalm shifts to family life. *"Children are a heritage from the Lord, offspring a reward from him."* Rather than seeing children as burdens or economic challenges, Solomon calls them blessings - gifts from God. Like arrows in the hands of a warrior, children are valuable and influential. A man with many children *"will not be put to shame when they contend with their opponents in court."*

This Psalm ties together work, rest, and family under one overarching truth: without God, we strive in vain. But with God, even ordinary things become blessed.

Key Verse: (v.1)
"Unless the Lord builds the house, the builders labour in vain."

Application:
Psalm 127 challenges us to evaluate the foundation of our efforts. Are we building our lives with God, or apart from Him? Commit your work, family, and plans to the Lord. He alone gives success that matters, and rest that restores. Trust in His timing and receive His blessings with gratitude.

PSALM 128

Author: Unknown

Theme: Blessing flows from fearing the Lord.

Summary:

Psalm 128 continues the wisdom theme, describing the blessings that come from living in reverent obedience to God. *"Blessed are all who fear the Lord, who walk in obedience to him."* The fear of the Lord isn't dread - it's respectful awe that shapes behaviour. This Psalm shows how such a life brings flourishing in both personal and communal spheres. The first blessing described is personal provision: *"You will eat the fruit of your labour; blessings and prosperity will be yours."* God honours the work of those who trust Him. This isn't a promise of luxury, but of satisfying provision.

The Psalm then moves to family: *"Your wife will be like a fruitful vine within your house; your children will be like olive shoots around your table."* The image is one of life, growth, and peace within the home. A family rooted in godliness flourishes like a well-tended garden. From personal to national, the Psalm expands its scope: *"May the Lord bless you from Zion; may you see the prosperity of Jerusalem all the days of your life."* The blessings of obedience are not isolated - they ripple outward into the community and nation. The final line is a prayer across generations: *"May you live to see your children's children - peace be on Israel."* It's a vision of enduring blessing grounded in reverence for God.

Key Verse: (v.1)

"Blessed are all who fear the Lord, who walk in obedience to him."

Application:

Psalm 128 is a portrait of a life well-lived in God's favour. It reminds us that reverence for God is not only right - it's rewarding. Walk in His ways, and you'll experience blessings that touch every corner of life. This is not prosperity gospel - it's a promise of God's faithful presence and provision.

PSALM 129

Author: Unknown

Theme: Confidence in God despite prolonged suffering.

Summary:

Psalm 129 is a gritty Psalm of perseverance. *"They have greatly oppressed me from my youth,"* begins the voice of Israel. This is a people who have known hardship from the beginning, whether in Egypt, the wilderness, or through enemy invasions. Yet despite the intensity of their suffering, they declare, *"they have not gained the victory over me."*

The Psalm uses harsh imagery: *"Ploughmen have ploughed my back and made their furrows long."* This speaks of deep wounds - literal or figurative - inflicted by enemies. But the hope remains: *"The Lord is righteous; he has cut me free from the cords of the wicked."* The oppressors tried to bind and break Israel, but God intervened.

Verses 5-8 contain a prayer for justice: *"May all who hate Zion be turned back in shame."* The Psalmist uses the metaphor of grass on a rooftop - short-lived and withering - to describe the fate of the wicked.

Their influence is brief, and they will not be remembered with blessing. This Psalm acknowledges pain but does not end in defeat. The righteous suffer, but they are not overcome.

Key Verse: (v.4)

"The Lord is righteous; he has cut me free from the cords of the wicked."

Application:

Psalm 129 reminds us that being God's people doesn't mean avoiding suffering. It means enduring with hope. God sees our afflictions and acts with justice. If you feel attacked or worn down, hold fast - oppression will not have the final word. God's deliverance is sure, even if it takes time.

PSALM 130

Author: Unknown

Theme: A cry for mercy and a confident
hope in God's forgiveness.

Summary:

Psalm 130 is one of the great penitential Psalms and a powerful
prayer for mercy, hope, and redemption. It begins from a place
of deep personal anguish: *"Out of the depths I cry to you, Lord."*
The depths suggest overwhelming sorrow or guilt - possibly
both - yet he does not turn inward - he cries upward to God. He
pleads, *"Lord, hear my voice. Let your ears be attentive to my cry for
mercy."* The next verses highlight an astonishing truth: *"If you,
Lord, kept a record of sins, Lord, who could stand?"* But the Psalm
takes a dramatic turn: *"But with you there is forgiveness, so that we
can, with reverence, serve you."* This forgiveness is not offered so
we can continue in sin but so we can revere and serve the Lord.

Then comes a beautiful picture of expectant faith: *"I wait for the
Lord, my whole being waits, and in his word I put my hope."* Waiting
here is not passive - it's a deep, soul-level longing. The Psalm
shifts from the individual to the nation: *"Israel, put your hope in
the Lord."* What began as a personal cry becomes a communal
invitation. *"For with the Lord is unfailing love and with him is full
redemption."* this is not theoretical: *"He himself will redeem Israel
from all their sins."* It's a promise anchored in God's character.

Key Verse: (vv.3-4)

*"If you, Lord, kept a record of sins, Lord, who could stand? But with
you there is forgiveness."*

Application:

Psalm 130 offers hope to every person burdened by sin or failure.
If you feel like you're in the depths, know that God hears. Cry
out. Trust in His unfailing love and wait expectantly. His
forgiveness is real, His redemption is complete, and His timing
is perfect. With God, there is always hope.

PSALM 131

Author: David

Theme: Humble trust and spiritual contentment.

Summary:

Psalm 131 is one of the shortest Psalms in the Bible but carries immense depth. Written by David, it reflects the heart of a man who has learned to rest in God's will without striving for position or control. *"My heart is not proud, Lord, my eyes are not haughty."* David declares that he has renounced arrogance and spiritual ambition.

The tone of the Psalm is gentle, calm, and profoundly mature. *"I do not concern myself with great matters or things too wonderful for me."* David has come to terms with the mystery of God's providence. He no longer needs to have all the answers. He is content to trust.

The central image of the Psalm is striking: *"But I have calmed and quieted myself, I am like a weaned child with its mother."* A weaned child no longer cries for milk but rests contentedly in the presence of their mother. This picture of spiritual maturity shows a believer who no longer relates to God simply for what He provides, but for who He is.

The Psalm ends with an exhortation: *"Israel, put your hope in the Lord both now and forevermore."* David invites the entire nation to enter into the same posture of peace, humility, and trust.

Key Verse: (v.2)

"I have calmed and quieted myself, I am like a weaned child with its mother."

Application:

Psalm 131 challenges us to embrace humility and rest. We often live in anxious striving - trying to control, understand, or fix things beyond us. This Psalm invites us to lay that down. Quiet your soul. Let go of spiritual pride. Trust the Lord not just for outcomes, but as your all-sufficient source.

PSALM 132

Author: Unknown

Theme: God's covenant with David and the blessings of His dwelling.

Summary:

Psalm 132 is the longest of the Songs of Ascents and a deeply historical Psalm, focusing on David's devotion to God and God's covenant with David. It begins by recalling David's vow: *"He swore an oath to the Lord... 'I will not enter my house... till I find a place for the Lord.'"* David's consuming passion was to establish a permanent dwelling place for the Ark of the Covenant. The Psalm references the Ark's movements: *"We heard it in Ephrathah... let us go to his dwelling place."*

God responds with promises that go beyond David's time: *"The Lord swore an oath to David, a sure oath he will not revoke: 'One of your own descendants I will place on your throne.'"* This looks ahead to the messianic promise - ultimately fulfilled in Jesus Christ.

The latter portion celebrates Zion as the chosen dwelling place of God. *"This is my resting place forever and ever."* Blessings are promised: abundant provision, salvation for the poor, joy for the faithful, and a crown for David's line. God says, *"Here I will make a horn grow for David,"* symbolizing strength and enduring rule.

Key Verse: (v.11)
"The Lord swore an oath to David... 'One of your own descendants I will place on your throne.'"

Application:
Psalm 132 reminds us that God honours faithfulness and keeps His promises. David's zeal to honour God was met with a covenant that extended to future generations. God still dwells among His people - not in temples, but in our hearts through Christ. Keep trusting God's promises. His plans are always bigger and longer lasting than ours.

PSALM 133

Author: David

Theme: The beauty and blessing of unity among God's people.

Summary:

Psalm 133 is a short but profound celebration of unity within the community of God's people. David begins with an exclamation: *"How good and pleasant it is when God's people live together in unity!"* The Psalm offers two vivid images. First, unity is *"like precious oil poured on the head, running down on the beard, running down on Aaron's beard, down on the collar of his robe."* When God's people dwell in unity, it reflects that sacred moment.

Second, unity is *"as if the dew of Hermon were falling on Mount Zion."* Mount Hermon, known for its refreshing dew, was far from Zion and geographically different. Yet the imagery conveys that unity brings unexpected and supernatural refreshment. What is distant and rare can be brought near and abundant through God's blessing. When God's people walk together in peace, spiritual vitality flows, just as dew nourishes the land.

The Psalm ends with this powerful conclusion: *"For there the Lord bestows his blessing, even life forevermore."* Unity is not just nice - it is essential. It is the atmosphere in which God commands blessing. When believers live in peace and love, God responds with life-giving grace.

Key Verse: (v.1)
"How good and pleasant it is when God's people live together in unity!"

Application:

Psalm 133 calls us to pursue unity as a sacred gift. Disagreements may happen, but division need not. Unity is forged through humility, forgiveness, shared purpose, and love. It is one of the most powerful testimonies of God's presence among His people. When believers stand together, heaven touches earth, and God's blessing flows.

PSALM 134

Author: Unknown

Theme: Night-time worship and reciprocal blessing.

Summary:

Psalm 134, the final of the Songs of Ascents, may be short in verse but is rich in meaning. It serves as a kind of benediction — a final encouragement for faithful worship. *"Praise the Lord, all you servants of the Lord who minister by night in the house of the Lord."* This greeting is directed to the priests and Levites who stood watch and ministered in the temple through the night hours. It's a reminder that worship isn't reserved for public gatherings; it continues in solitude and stillness. God is no less worthy of praise when no one is watching.

"Lift up your hands in the sanctuary and praise the Lord." This call is both physical and spiritual. Lifting hands was a posture of surrender, blessing, and honour. It's a way of saying, *"All I am belongs to You."* Even in the silent, dark hours, God's people are encouraged to engage with Him in reverent awe.

The Psalm concludes with a reciprocal blessing: *"May the Lord bless you from Zion, he who is the Maker of heaven and earth."* As the people bless God with their worship, God blesses them in return. The God who created the universe chooses to dwell in Zion, to meet with His people in tangible ways.

Key Verse: (v.3)

"May the Lord bless you from Zion, he who is the Maker of heaven and earth."

Application:

Psalm 134 encourages us to remain faithful in worship, even when it feels quiet or unnoticed. God sees what is done in secret and honours devotion that persists through the night. Whether in public praise or private prayer, our worship matters. Lift your hands to God - not for show, but in surrender - and receive the blessing He delights to give.

PSALM 135

Author: Unknown

Theme: Praising the greatness of God over idols.

Summary:

Psalm 135 is a powerful call to praise, rooted in the unmatched greatness of God. *"Praise the Lord. Praise the name of the Lord; praise him, you servants of the Lord."* It begins with those who minister in God's house - calling them to lift up His name because *"the Lord is good"* and *"his name endures forever."* The Psalm praises God's sovereignty in choosing Israel and controlling nature: *"The Lord does whatever pleases him, in the heavens and on the earth."* From lifting vapours to releasing lightning, God governs the world with unmatched authority.

A significant portion is devoted to remembering God's saving acts - especially in Egypt and the wilderness. *"He struck down many nations and killed mighty kings."* These historical reminders reinforce God's role as both deliverer and judge. In contrast to the living God, the Psalm mocks idols: *"They have mouths, but cannot speak, eyes, but cannot see."* They are lifeless and powerless, and *"those who make them will be like them."* Worship shapes us - those who trust in idols become spiritually dead.

The Psalm ends with a chorus of blessings: all who fear the Lord - house of Israel, house of Aaron, house of Levi - are called to bless His name.

Key Verse: (v.6)

"The Lord does whatever pleases him, in the heavens and on the earth."

Application:

Psalm 135 is a vivid reminder that our God is alive, powerful, and worthy of all praise. Unlike idols that promise much but do nothing, the Lord speaks, acts, and saves. Reflect on His greatness today. Worship not just with words, but with trust, obedience, and joy. Let your life praise the living God.

PSALM 136

Author: Unknown
Theme: God's steadfast love endures forever.

Summary:
Psalm 136 is a majestic hymn of praise that recounts the mighty acts of God in creation, deliverance, and provision. Each verse ends with the identical refrain: *"His love endures forever."* This repetition reinforces the central truth of the Psalm - that God's steadfast, covenantal love is eternal and unfailing. It begins with a threefold call to give thanks to God: to the Lord, to the God of gods, and to the Lord of lords. These titles affirm His supreme sovereignty and authority over all of creation.

The Psalm then moves into a poetic recounting of God's work. *"To him who alone does great wonders,"* refers to the marvels of creation - spreading out the earth, placing the stars, sun, and moon in their courses - all evidence of His loving design.

The Psalm then shifts to God's historical acts, focusing on the deliverance of Israel from Egypt. It recalls the plagues, the Passover, the parting of the Red Sea, and the destruction of Pharaoh's army. *"To him who struck down the firstborn of Egypt… and brought Israel out from among them."* The Psalm also highlights God's ongoing care: *"He remembered us in our low estate… and freed us from our enemies."* The final verses return to creation and provision: "He gives food to every creature." This universal care shows that God's love is not only for Israel but extends to us all.

Key Verse: (v.1)
"Give thanks to the Lord, for he is good. His love endures forever."

Application:
Psalm 136 reminds us to ground our faith in the unchanging love of God. In every moment - creation, crisis, victory, provision - His love endures. Let this refrain shape your heart and prayers. No matter your circumstances, God's love has not run out. Give thanks with confidence. His mercy surrounds you, always.

PSALM 137

Author: Unknown

Theme: Lament in exile and longing for justice.

Summary:

Psalm 137 is one of the most emotionally raw Psalms in the Bible. It captures the pain of exile, the heartbreak of loss, and the desperate cry for justice. *"By the rivers of Babylon we sat and wept when we remembered Zion."* The people of Judah, taken captive by Babylon, sit in sorrow by foreign waters, mourning their beloved Jerusalem. The Psalm is filled with images of grief and humiliation. The captors demand a song: *"Sing us one of the songs of Zion!"* But the people cannot bring themselves to rejoice in a strange land. *"How can we sing the songs of the Lord while in a foreign land?"* Their music has turned to mourning.

In a powerful act of spiritual resolve, the Psalmist declares, *"If I forget you, Jerusalem, may my right hand forget its skill."* Even in exile, the memory of God's city remains central. This is not just nationalistic sentiment - it reflects deep spiritual yearning. The Psalm ends with a jarring plea for justice. It calls upon God to remember the Edomites who cheered Jerusalem's destruction and petitions judgment against Babylon: *"Blessed is the one who repays you for what you have done to us."* These are not instructions for personal revenge but cries for divine justice, born from intense suffering.

Key Verse: (v.4)

"How can we sing the songs of the Lord while in a foreign land?"

Application:

Psalm 137 teaches us to bring our sorrow and anger honestly before God. In seasons of exile - when life feels foreign and broken - lament is a faithful response. God welcomes our grief, our questions, and even our longing for justice. Hold fast to your spiritual identity, and trust that the Lord sees and will act in righteousness.

PSALM 138

Author: David

Theme: Gratitude and confidence in God's faithfulness.

Summary:

Psalm 138 is a joyful declaration of thanksgiving from David, celebrating God's unfailing love and truth. *"I will praise you, Lord, with all my heart."* David is not offering half-hearted thanks - his praise is total and undivided. He is even willing to worship before other *"gods,"* a way of saying that no rival power can deter his devotion to the one true God. David gives thanks because God has answered him: *"When I called, you answered me; you greatly emboldened me."* The Lord's responsiveness has strengthened David's soul and stirred bold confidence.

The Psalm envisions a day when *"all the kings of the earth"* will praise God when they hear His words. This hope reflects David's confidence that God's truth and glory will one day be universally recognized. Even though the Lord is exalted, *"he looks kindly on the lowly,"* showing that God's greatness never distances Him from human need.

David expresses assurance even in hardship: *"Though I walk in the midst of trouble, you preserve my life."* The Psalm ends with this powerful promise: *"The Lord will vindicate me; your love, Lord, endures forever - do not abandon the works of your hands."* David trusts that God's purpose for him will be fulfilled.

Key Verse: (v.8)

"The Lord will vindicate me; your love, Lord, endures forever."

Application:

Psalm 138 urges us to be people of gratitude and trust. God hears, responds, and strengthens us in trouble. Praise Him not only for what He has done, but for who He is. When your path is hard, remember that God is not distant. He is near, faithful, and will complete the work He began in you.

PSALM 139

Author: David

Theme: God's intimate knowledge,
presence, and creative power.

Summary:

Psalm 139 is a deeply personal reflection on the omniscience, omnipresence, and creative involvement of God. The Psalm begins with the declaration, *"You have searched me, Lord, and you know me."* God's knowledge of David isn't casual or distant - it is penetrating and complete. He knows David's every move, every word before it's spoken, and every unformed thought. *"Such knowledge is too wonderful for me, too lofty for me to attain."* David marvels at the fact that there is nowhere he can go to escape God's presence. *"Where can I go from your Spirit? Where can I flee from your presence?"* The answer is nowhere.

The Psalm then celebrates God's intricate involvement in human creation. *"You created my inmost being; you knit me together in my mother's womb."* David is acknowledging the divine hand behind every life. *"I praise you because I am fearfully and wonderfully made."* Our identities are not accidents; they are authored by God Himself. David then reflects on God's eternal plan: *"All the days ordained for me were written in your book before one of them came to be."* This affirms divine sovereignty and personal significance.

The Psalm ends with a heartfelt desire for purity and alignment with God's will. *"Search me, God, and know my heart; test me and know my anxious thoughts."*

Key Verse:

"You have searched me, Lord, and you know me."

Application:

Psalm 139 reminds us that we are never out of God's sight, reach, or care. He knows you fully - your flaws, fears, and future - and He still loves you. You are not hidden, forgotten, or alone. Invite God to search your heart and lead you in His everlasting way.

PSALM 140

Author: David

Theme: Seeking God's protection.

Summary:

David begins with a clear and urgent plea: *"Rescue me, Lord, from evildoers; protect me from the violent."* He is surrounded by people who plan evil in their hearts. Their speech is poisonous and deadly - *"They make their tongues as sharp as a serpent's; the poison of vipers is on their lips."* The threats are not just verbal. David's enemies lay traps and snares for his downfall. *"They spread out the cords of their nets and set traps for me along my path."* The Psalm portrays a world filled with deceit, betrayal, and malice.

David addresses God directly: *"You are my God, hear the Lord my cry for mercy."* He expresses confidence in God's faithfulness and justice: *"Sovereign Lord, my strong deliverer, you shield my head in the day of battle."* The Psalm includes a bold plea for divine justice: *"Do not grant the wicked their desires, Lord; do not let their plans succeed."* David doesn't seek revenge on his own but trusts God.

David closes with reassurance: *"I know that the Lord secures justice for the poor and upholds the cause of the needy."* This is not wishful thinking - it's a declaration rooted in the character of God. The Psalm ends in confident hope: *"Surely the righteous will praise your name, and the upright will live in your presence."*

Key Verse: (v.7)

"Sovereign Lord, my strong deliverer, you shield my head in the day of battle."

Application:

Psalm 140 encourages us to turn to God when evil surrounds us. Whether facing slander, injustice, or spiritual opposition, we can rest in God's protection and justice. Don't be overcome by the presence of evil - be sustained by the presence of God. He is your shield, your defender, and your righteous Judge.

PSALM 141

Author: David

Theme: A cry for purity, protection, and godly influence.

Summary:

Psalm 141 is a deeply personal prayer by David, offered during a time of pressure and temptation. He begins with urgency: *"I call to you, Lord, come quickly to me."* David longs for God's immediate attention and intervention, desiring that his prayer would be as incense - pleasing and acceptable to the Lord. *"May my prayer be set before you like incense; may the lifting up of my hands be like the evening sacrifice."* David knows that external threats are not the only danger - his own heart can be a battlefield. He prays, *"Set a guard over my mouth, Lord; keep watch over the door of my lips."* He doesn't want his words to betray his commitment to righteousness. He also asks God to protect him from being drawn into evil actions, saying, *"Do not let my heart be drawn to what is evil so that I take part in wicked deeds."*

Interestingly, David welcomes correction from the godly: *"Let a righteous man strike me - that is a kindness."* He understands that accountability and wise rebuke are part of staying faithful. David speaks of enemies who set traps for him, yet he remains confident that the Lord will preserve him: *"But my eyes are fixed on you, Sovereign Lord; in you I take refuge - do not give me over to death."* He ends with a plea that the wicked will fall into their own nets while he passes by safely.

Key Verse: (v.8)

"But my eyes are fixed on you, Sovereign Lord; in you I take refuge - do not give me over to death."

Application:

Psalm 141 challenges us to pray for inner purity, not just external protection. In a world filled with spiritual compromise, we need God's help to speak truth, resist temptation, and stay humble. Be open to correction from godly people. And keep your eyes fixed on the Lord - He is your refuge and strength.

PSALM 142

Author: David

Theme: A cry for help from a lonely soul.

Summary:

Psalm 142 is a heartfelt plea from David while hiding in a cave - likely during his flight from Saul. It is labelled *"a maskil of David. When he was in the cave."* This setting gives the Psalm emotional weight. David is not in a palace or temple, but in hiding, isolated and vulnerable. *"I cry aloud to the Lord; I lift up my voice to the Lord for mercy."*

David's prayer is raw and honest. He pours out his complaint and expresses his trouble without holding back. *"When my spirit grows faint within me, it is you who watch over my way."* Even in darkness and confusion, David affirms that God sees and cares. He feels utterly alone: *"Look and see, there is no one at my right hand; no one is concerned for me."* His enemies are too strong, and his companions too few.

Yet David does not sink into despair. He turns his attention to the Lord: *"I cry to you, Lord; I say, 'You are my refuge, my portion in the land of the living.'"* David pleads for deliverance, asking God to free him from his prison of fear and isolation. He desires not only relief but the opportunity to praise God openly and publicly again. *"Set me free from my prison, that I may praise your name."*

Key Verse: (v.5)

"I cry to you, Lord; I say, 'You are my refuge, my portion in the land of the living.'"

Application:

Psalm 142 reminds us that in moments of isolation, fear, or despair, we can still cry out to God. He listens, even from the cave. When others abandon us, the Lord remains. Let your trials drive you to deeper dependence on Him. He is your refuge, your portion, and your deliverer.

PSALM 143

Author: David

Theme: Seeking God's mercy and guidance in times of distress.

Summary:

Psalm 143 is one of David's penitential Psalms - a blend of confession, lament, and plea for mercy. It opens with a humble cry: *"Lord, hear my prayer, listen to my cry for mercy."* David does not demand God's help on the basis of his righteousness but appeals to God's faithfulness and justice. He acknowledges that no one can stand before God on their own merit: *"Do not bring your servant into judgment, for no one living is righteous before you."* This is a powerful statement of human fallibility and the need for grace. His spirit is crushed: *"The enemy pursues me... he makes me dwell in the darkness like those long dead."*

Yet David fights this despair with remembrance: *"I remember the days of long ago; I meditate on all your works."* Recalling God's past faithfulness becomes his source of hope. David thirsts for God like parched land. *"I spread out my hands to you; I thirst for you like a parched land."* He pleads for a quick answer before he gives way to hopelessness. *"Let the morning bring me word of your unfailing love, for I have put my trust in you."* He asks for guidance: *"Show me the way I should go... Teach me to do your will."* This Psalm ends not with resolution but with deep surrender. David entrusts his soul to God, asking to be rescued, revived, and led by the Spirit.

Key Verse: (v.8)

"Let the morning bring me word of your unfailing love, for I have put my trust in you."

Application:

Psalm 143 encourages us to seek God in times of guilt, confusion, and distress. Admit your weakness, remember His faithfulness, and ask Him to guide you forward. Like David, thirst for God's presence. He is merciful to the broken and faithful to lead those who trust in Him.

PSALM 144

Author: David

Theme: God's power in battle and His blessing in peace.

Summary:

David begins by praising God as his warrior-king: *"Praise be to the Lord my Rock, who trains my hands for war, my fingers for battle."* God is the source of strength and skill, the One who equips His people for the conflicts of life. David acknowledges God not only as a military ally but also as *"my loving God and my fortress, my stronghold and my deliverer."* Despite this bold beginning, David humbles himself: *"Lord, what are human beings that you care for them, mere mortals that you think of them?"*

He cries out for help: *"Part your heavens, Lord, and come down; touch the mountains, so that they smoke."* David seeks deliverance from enemies who speak falsehoods and deal deceitfully. *"I will sing a new song to you, my God… you deliver your servant David."* The Psalm then shifts to a vision of peace and prosperity. David prays for the flourishing of future generations: *"Our sons in their youth will be like well-nurtured plants, and our daughters will be like pillars carved to adorn a palace."* He imagines barns filled with produce, sheep multiplying by the thousands, and people living without fear or sorrow.

The Psalm concludes with a resounding declaration: *"Blessed is the people of whom this is true; blessed is the people whose God is the Lord."*

Key Verse: (v.15)

"Blessed is the people whose God is the Lord."

Application:

Psalm 144 encourages us to rely on God for strength in battle and to seek His blessing in times of peace. We must acknowledge our weakness and turn to Him for help, whether we are under attack or enjoying prosperity. Security is found not in weapons or wealth, but in worship and relationship with the Lord.

PSALM 145

Author: David

Theme: A majestic and eternal praise to God's character.

Summary:
Psalm 145 is both personal and universal, expressing heartfelt worship and inviting all creation to join in exalting God. David begins with intention: *"I will exalt you, my God the King; I will praise your name for ever and ever."* His praise is not confined to a moment but pledged for a lifetime and beyond. He continues, *"Great is the Lord and most worthy of praise; his greatness no one can fathom."* David then emphasizes generational testimony: *"One generation commends your works to another; they tell of your mighty acts."* He praises God's abundant goodness and righteousness. *"The Lord is gracious and compassionate, slow to anger and rich in love."* This statement echoes God's self-revelation to Moses and becomes a theological anchor throughout the Old Testament.

The Psalm moves from personal praise to cosmic recognition. *"The Lord is trustworthy in all he promises and faithful in all he does."* He upholds those who fall, satisfies the desires of every living thing, and hears the cries of those who call on Him. His nearness is not reserved for the elite - it is extended to *"all who call on him in truth."* David concludes with certainty: *"The Lord watches over all who love him, but all the wicked he will destroy."* The Psalm ends with personal commitment: *"My mouth will speak in praise of the Lord. Let every creature praise his holy name for ever and ever."*

Key Verse: (v.8)
"The Lord is gracious and compassionate, slow to anger and rich in love."

Application:
Psalm 145 invites us to make worship a way of life. Reflect often on God's goodness, share His deeds with the next generation, and celebrate His grace. He is both near and mighty, just and compassionate. Let every word and action point others to His greatness and let your life become a song of praise.

PSALM 146

Author: Anonymous

Theme: Trust in God, not in man.

Summary:

Psalm 146 begins a crescendo of praise that continues through the final five Psalms. It opens with joyful resolution: *"Praise the Lord. Praise the Lord, my soul."* This personal exhortation reminds us that worship starts within. The Psalmist declares, *"I will praise the Lord all my life; I will sing praise to my God as long as I live."* Worship is not reserved for a moment but is the theme of life. The Psalm immediately warns against misplaced trust: *"Do not put your trust in princes, in human beings, who cannot save."* No matter how powerful or influential a person may seem, they are mortal. *"When their spirit departs, they return to the ground; on that very day their plans come to nothing."*

The Psalmist points to the blessedness of those who trust in the Lord: *"Blessed are those whose help is the God of Jacob."* Why? Because God is the eternal Creator of heaven, earth, and sea, and He remains faithful forever. He is not limited like man - He upholds justice, feeds the hungry, frees the prisoner, and gives sight to the blind. The Lord lifts up those who are bowed down and loves the righteous. He watches over the foreigner, sustains the fatherless and the widow, and frustrates the plans of the wicked. His reign is eternal: *"The Lord reigns forever, your God, O Zion, for all generations."*

Key Verse: (v.3)

"Do not put your trust in princes, in human beings, who cannot save."

Application:

Psalm 146 calls us to shift our trust from human institutions and leaders to the living God. People fail, but God is faithful. Make Him your help, your hope, and your praise. Let your worship be lifelong, and your confidence be rooted in the One who reigns.

PSALM 147

Author: Anonymous

Theme: God's greatness in power and tenderness.

Summary:

Psalm 147 celebrates God's majesty alongside His mercy. *"Praise the Lord. How good it is to sing praises to our God, how pleasant and fitting to praise him!"* Worship is not only a duty - it is a delight. This Psalm shows that the One who numbers the stars also heals the broken-hearted. God is praised as the rebuilder of Jerusalem and the gatherer of Israel's exiles. He heals wounds and binds up the broken. His greatness is not only measured by power - *"His understanding has no limit"* - but also by His compassion. *"The Lord sustains the humble but casts the wicked to the ground."*

The Psalm invites us to worship through nature. God covers the sky with clouds, prepares rain, makes grass grow, and provides food for animals. Yet He is not impressed by human strength: *"His pleasure is not in the strength of the horse… but the Lord delights in those who fear him."* Reverence matters more than might.

Jerusalem is again called to praise. God strengthens its gates, blesses its people, and brings peace within its borders. He sends His word, commands the elements, and governs the seasons. His word melts ice and sends flowing waters. The Psalm ends with a declaration of privilege: *"He has revealed his word to Jacob… He has done this for no other nation."*

Key Verse: (v.3)

"He heals the broken-hearted and binds up their wounds."

Application:

Psalm 147 reminds us that God is both powerful and personal. He governs galaxies and yet heals wounded hearts. Worship Him not only for His strength, but for His care. Fear Him, trust Him, and take comfort in His sustaining grace. He delights in those who revere His name.

PSALM 148

Author: Anonymous

Theme: All creation called to praise the Lord.

Summary:

Psalm 148 is a sweeping call to praise, summoning every part of creation to glorify the Lord. It begins with an upward gaze: *"Praise the Lord from the heavens; praise him in the heights above."* Heavenly beings - angels, sun, moon, stars, and celestial waters - are urged to declare His glory. These entities were created by God and remain fixed by His sovereign decree. *"He set them in place for ever and ever; he gave a decree that will never pass away."*

Then the focus shifts from heaven to earth: *"Praise the Lord from the earth."* But the invitation to praise is not limited to the non-human world. Humanity is summoned next - *"kings of the earth and all nations, you princes and all rulers on earth, young men and women, old men and children."* No one is exempt. God stands infinitely above everything He has made, yet He is not distant. *"He has raised up for his people a horn"* - a symbol of strength and salvation - referring perhaps to His anointed king or the Messiah.

The Psalm concludes by affirming God's nearness to His people: *"The praise of all his faithful servants, of Israel, the people close to his heart."* This universal chorus finds its centre in a personal relationship between the Creator and His covenant people.
his splendour is above the earth and the heavens."

Key Verse: (v.13)
"Let them praise the name of the Lord, for his name alone is exalted; his splendour is above the earth and the heavens."

Application:

Psalm 148 challenges us to join the universal chorus of praise that surrounds the throne of God. Worship isn't confined to humans or places of worship - it reverberates through nature, time, and space. If the stars and storms praise Him, how much more should we who bear His image?

PSALM 149

Author: Anonymous

Theme: Joyful worship and readiness for spiritual battle.

Summary:

Psalm 149 is a dynamic mixture of worship, celebration, and spiritual readiness. It begins with a command: *"Praise the Lord. Sing to the Lord a new song, his praise in the assembly of his faithful people."* This new song is not merely a fresh melody - it signifies a renewed encounter with God and His works.

The people of God are encouraged to rejoice in their Maker and King, engaging in expressive and physical worship. *"Let them praise his name with dancing and make music to him with timbrel and harp."* This vibrant celebration is rooted in a profound truth: *"For the Lord takes delight in his people; he crowns the humble with victory."* God is not distant or indifferent - He delights in His people.

The Psalm takes a surprising turn in the second half. God's faithful people are described as warriors: *"May the praise of God be in their mouths and a double-edged sword in their hands."* While literal violence is not the focus, this imagery reflects a readiness to engage in spiritual battle. It points to the dignity and authority bestowed upon God's people to live out His purposes in the world. The Psalm ends as it began: *"Praise the Lord."* Worship, justice, celebration, and courage are all woven together in the life of the faithful.

Key Verse: (v.4)

"For the Lord takes delight in his people; he crowns the humble with victory."

Application:

Psalm 149 reminds us that joyful worship and spiritual courage go hand in hand. Celebrate God with gladness, knowing He delights in you. At the same time, be spiritually alert and willing to stand for truth and righteousness. Let your worship empower your witness and let your praise overflow into action.

PSALM 150

Author: Anonymous

Theme: A climactic call to universal praise.

Summary:

Psalm 150 is the climactic conclusion to the Book of Psalms. It contains no lament, no petition, no narrative - only unfiltered praise. It opens and closes with the same word: *"Praise the Lord."* This Psalm is a call to worship with abandonment, encompassing every instrument, every setting, and every living thing. *"Praise God in his sanctuary; praise him in his mighty heavens."* The Psalm begins with a call to worship both in the temple and in the vast reaches of creation.

It then gives us the reason: *"Praise him for his acts of power; praise him for his surpassing greatness."* Worship flows not only from what God does - His mighty acts - but also from who He is - His infinite greatness. These two truths form the foundation of all praise. The instruments of worship are then listed: trumpet, harp, lyre, timbrel, strings, pipe, and cymbals - both loud and resounding. This rich variety reminds us that worship is not confined to one style or form.

The final verse is sweeping and inclusive: *"Let everything that has breath praise the Lord."* No voice is too small, no life too insignificant. All of creation is summoned to lift its breath in praise. It is both a command and an invitation - to use every breath for the glory of God.

Key Verse: (v.6)

"Let everything that has breath praise the Lord. Praise the Lord."

Application:

Psalm 150 challenges us to live lives filled with praise. Worship isn't reserved for musicians or certain places - it belongs to everyone who has breath. Use your voice, your gifts, your time, and your breath to honour God. Let praise be your response to His greatness and your rhythm through every season of life.

CONCLUSION

You have now journeyed through 150 sacred songs that span the full range of human experience. In these pages, you have read cries of anguish and shouts of triumph, heartfelt repentance and exuberant praise, lonely pleas and communal celebrations. From the darkness of the valley to the joy of the mountaintop, the Psalms have walked with you and pointed your heart to God.

These songs were meant for every generation, every culture and every soul that seeks to know God more deeply. The Psalms invite us to be honest before the Lord - to bring our questions, our tears, our failures, and our dreams to Him without fear. They remind us that faith is not the absence of struggle but the resolve to trust God in the midst of any and every circumstance.

We have seen God revealed as Creator, Shepherd, King, Refuge, Rock, and Redeemer. We have encountered His justice, mercy, patience, and power. The Psalms show us a God who is both high and holy, yet near to the broken-hearted. He listens, He answers, and He delivers.

The Psalms teach us how to worship with awe, to lament with honesty, to hope with confidence, and to obey with joy. They have shown us that God's Word is a lamp to our feet and a light to our path. They have encouraged us to meditate on His Word, trust in His timing, and rest in His promises.

But this journey is not meant to end here. The Psalms are not just to be read - they are to be prayed, sung, and lived. Keep them close. Return to them often. Let their words become your own, especially in times when your own words fall short. Allow their rhythms to steady you, their truths to guide you, and their praises to lift you.

As you close this companion, may your heart remain open to the God it reveals. May you continue to grow in love, in trust, and in reverence. And may your life, like the final Psalm, be marked by one great theme: *"Let everything that has breath praise the Lord. Praise the Lord."* (Psalm 150:6)

www.ingramcontent.com/pod-product-compliance
Lightning Source LLC
Chambersburg PA
CBHW051737020426

42333CB00014B/1349